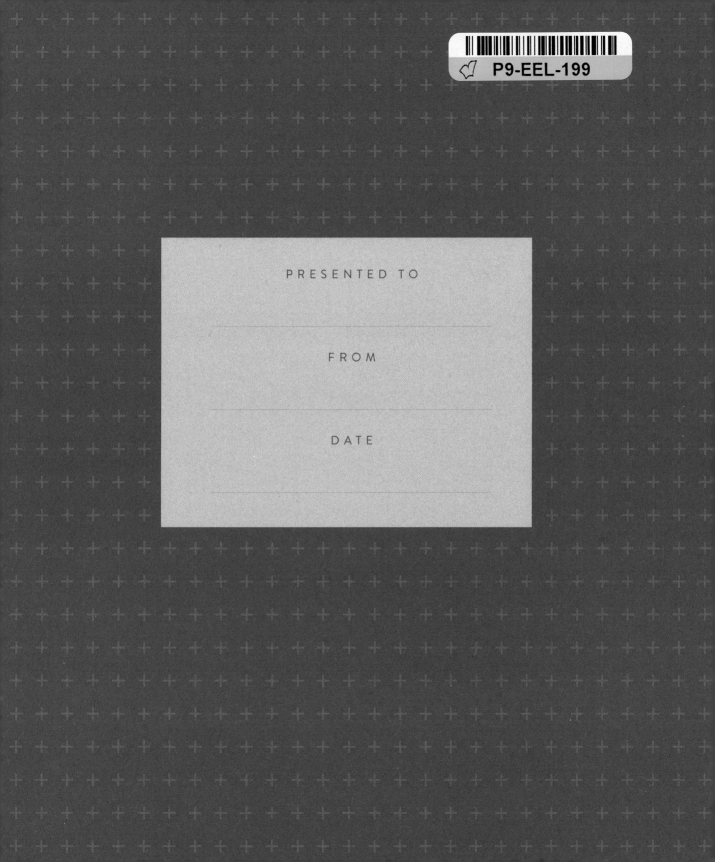

PRESENTED TO

FROM

DATE

PRAISE FOR *RESTORATION HOUSE*

"*Restoration House* is a must-read for anyone who longs to create a home with a greater purpose than simply looking pretty. Kennesha guides you through how the heart and soul of your home can reflect the heart and soul of your very life, and that makes all the difference. Make room on your coffee table for this beautiful book."

—MYQUILLYN SMITH, *Wall Street Journal* bestselling author of *Cozy Minimalist Home*

"I've noticed (and loved) two things in particular about Kennesha, her writing, and her work for the past few years: 1) everything she does is beautiful and reflects the beauty of God, and 2) her revolution around the word *restoration*. In a world obsessed with making everything flashy, tidy, and fake, I love the idea and the pursuit of restoration. I'm so thankful for her gentle leading toward it. Yes to restored homes, families, identities, and hearts. You'll love this book, you'll love Kennesha, and you'll love your own restored life a little more after reading it."

—JESS CONNOLLY, author of *Dance, Stand, Run* and *You Are the Girl for the Job* (September 2019) and coauthor of *Wild and Free* and *Always Enough, Never Too Much*

"I've always been homesick for nowhere in particular, at least nowhere I've ever called home. I'm guessing I'm not the only woman who could say that. For all of us, I'm glad Kennesha is here as a been-there-done-that ambassador to a home that is truly nourishing to our own souls and the souls of all who pass through our doors. What a hopeful and necessary perspective in a noisy and chaotic world!"

—HAYLEY MORGAN, author of *Preach to Yourself* and coauthor of *Wild and Free* and *Always Enough, Never Too Much*

"Kennesha has a beautiful way of creating magic with her words and with her spaces. The combination of the two has led to this stunning book, full of applicable design, wondrous design, and of course, restoring design. This will be in your design library for forever!"

—KIRSTEN GROVE, author of *Simply Styling* and the *Simply Grove* blog

"Maya Angelou said what our hearts long for most: "The ache for home lives in all of us, the safe place where we can go as we are and not be questioned." Home is supposed to be a safe place—where we go to be seen, heard, refreshed, and restored. God makes His home in our hearts, and I believe He writes His story in our lives and in our homes so that, ultimately, those who enter will find rest and peace in Him. Kennesha has reminded us with this beautifully written book that home is more than its size, shape, and showmanship. It is a sacred space where we invite others in to celebrate, create memories, and experience the joy that is found in authentic living."

—TARA LOWRY, creator of Between You and Me Signs

RESTORATION HOUSE

CREATING A SPACE THAT GIVES LIFE AND CONNECTION TO ALL WHO ENTER

KENNESHA BUYCKS

PHOTOGRAPHY BY TIARRA SORTE

ZONDERVAN

Restoration House

Copyright © 2019 by Kennesha Buycks

Requests for information should be addressed to:

Zondervan, *3900 Sparks Dr. SE, Grand Rapids, MI 49546*

ISBN 978-0-3100-9206-3

Author is represented by the literary agency of The Fedd Agency, Inc., P. O. Box 341973, Austin, Texas 78734.

Photography: Tiarra Sorte
Art direction: Adam Hill
Interior design: Lori Lynch

Printed in China

19 20 21 22 23 DSC 11 10 9 8 7 6 5 4 3 2

CONTENTS

INTRODUCTION

I n our first ten years of marriage, we moved almost ten times. Many things have changed for us since our first move into a tiny studio apartment. The things that I dreamed of and desired as a naive twenty-two-year-old newlywed are not the same things that are important to me now that I am well into my thirties. While we are far from wealthy (at least in the physical sense), we are beyond rich in seeing the faithfulness and goodness of God fulfilled in our lives. We've been able, in every season—no matter the home—to find respite, retreat, and His restoration plan fulfilled.

God is good. There hasn't been a time I've uttered the name *Restoration House* without being reminded of that simple yet profound truth. Restoration has been a consistent message and theme throughout my writing and the lifespan of my blog, RestorationHouseBlog.com, for the last ten years. As I have restored furniture and transformed rooms in my home, I have experienced God's restoration in every area of my life. I have watched as my own story of restoration has encouraged, inspired, and brought freedom to thousands of lives through my blog and social media.

You're probably wondering by now what all of this has to do with you.

Well, I believe there is an often silent part of each of us that continually searches for and demands more. In every one of us is an inherent, deeply felt need to feel at home; yet never before in history has our culture been more disconnected. We get lost in a sea of e-mails and text messages, meetings, social media, appointments, and obligations, and we wonder why we never feel at peace in our own homes. What we all desperately need is a place to reflect, restore, and reengage with the community God has given to each of us.

> What we all desperately need is a place to reflect, restore, and reengage with the community God has given to each of us.

God created us to live together—it's a huge part of our purpose. Women in particular are crying out for a restored sense of self and restored relationships with others, with every home design show we watch and seasonal throw pillow we buy. We all want to rediscover a sense of calm and renewal of purpose in our homes without feeling overwhelmed by the pressure to measure up to cultural standards.

The messages we see in media and online tell us that we are not good enough and that we will never measure up. Fearing rejection or judgment, we exclude ourselves before someone else can, and we shelter our hearts

What if the very space we close off
is the one place God intends to use as
a place of restoration in our own lives,
and in the lives of others?

and our homes. In the process, we ultimately shut down the one space God has given us to open up and share our lives: our homes.

What if the very space we close off is the one place God intends to use as a place of restoration in our own lives, and in the lives of others? What would happen if we put aside our fears and insecurities and decided to open our lives and homes in a way we never have before?

This book is about creating places and spaces where women can feel secure, connected, revived, and renewed. This place for me and, I believe, for you begins at home.

For the woman who dreams of creating a place that gives life to those who enter: this is for you. For the woman who envisions her home as a place of rest and retreat—not just for herself but for others—and may struggle with reaching that goal: this is for you. This book is for the one who believes she is lost and has been forgotten—the one whose life has lost purpose and the one who needs to be reminded that home is more than a mere space to be filled with pretty pillows and beautifully decorated walls. Yes, this book is for you. Extending our reach far beyond fine linens, fancy flatware, and expensive furniture, we will delve into how our homes can serve as places of restoration for ourselves, our families, and our communities.

Together we will overcome our fears and create spaces of restoration and connection to live as we were intended to live—a life more fulfilled, impactful, and meaningful because of those we invite in. ^{RH}

PART 1

RESTORED HOME, RESTORED SOUL

He makes me lie down in green pastures.
He leads me beside still waters.
He restores my soul.

—PSALM 23:2–3 ESV

CHAPTER 1

A PLACE TO RESTORE YOUR IDENTITY

By wisdom a house is built,
and through understanding it is established;
through knowledge its rooms are filled
with rare and beautiful treasures.

—PROVERBS 24:3–4

What does home mean to you? Popular culture tells us that the ideal home should be beautiful, calm, and warm. Home is supposed to be a place to recharge and retreat—a place of restoration. But for so many of us, home is far from that rosy ideal.

For better or for worse, our homes shape who we are and who we turn out to be. Our experiences with and in our homes have the power to mold us into contented, confident people or to keep us stuck in a rut.

If you're like me, you've lived long enough to have the full experience of both. Home should be a safe place where you can fully be yourself, shouldn't it? But what if it's not quite there yet? And what if no one's ever taught you how to take it there?

Friend, I want to take you by the hand and lead you toward a home that restores you—a home that goes beyond good-looking to life-bringing. Yes, God has given us an eternal home in Him that will always be safe, but we also have homes here on earth. I believe our homes give us the unique opportunity to echo the healing, restoration, joy, and redemption that our Creator so lovingly and freely gives. If God has renewed our identity in Him, we can celebrate and reflect it in the places we call home.

When we think about sprucing up our homes, I think most of us focus a lot on making them stylish or clean instead of how we can restore them to places that are life-giving to ourselves, to those we love, and to just about everyone who enters. Never mind making it *perfect*. Let's toss that word to the side for the rest of this book. Agreed? Deal.

If you look at my blog or my Instagram feed, you'll see beautiful pictures of my home and my family. It all looks pretty idyllic, huh? But home hasn't even come close to being a place of restoration for me for most of my life. As I'll share in the next chapter, my childhood home was a curious mixture of love and grief and loss. It wasn't a bad place most days, but it wasn't always a place where I could go to be restored. As I carried that unsettledness with me to every one of my adult homes, I found myself trying to create something in my home that I didn't really understand and had no idea how to tap into: *Peace. Connection. A place to be me.*

Year after year I searched for my identity in the things I placed in my home, not realizing no matter how much I filled my space with all the "good and pretty things," the hole in my heart was one that only God could fill. There was no curtain or pillow or paint color that could do that. But God was about to start rewriting the story, restoring the idea of home, starting inside me. He figuratively picked me up. In the midst of my searching, He used the unexpected vehicle of the military to bring more wholeness and healing than I could have ever imagined.

> No matter how much I filled my space with all the "good and pretty things," the hole in my heart was one that only God could fill.

A NEW PERSPECTIVE

My husband, Larry, served in the military for the first ten years of our marriage. We've lived in ten homes in seventeen years, so home is a concept I've been forced to revisit time and again with each moving-truck pickup. Our last home in the military was on the island of Oahu, Hawaii. It was the absolute dreamiest place to live for everyone in my family—except for me.

You see, I'd never lived that far away from my extended family and network of friends before. It was the first time that Larry and I moved to a location where we had no previous connection or relationships—no distant relatives to invite us to dinner, no friend of a friend of a friend

to show us around and help us meet new people. We were on our own, and all the puzzle pieces that I thought reflected identity, that reflected the core of who I really was and the purpose I was meant to serve, were suddenly pulled apart. I struggled to piece together what made me *me*. And us *us*.

It was also the first time in our then seven years of marriage that Larry and I *needed* to be that far away from everything we'd ever known. Our marriage and spiritual lives were in rough places, and I wasn't sure we'd be able to hold it together through one more move.

We had gotten married when we were young. Babies, some called us. We were completely clueless about what it took to have a healthy marriage. Who knew you actually had to *work* to make that happen? Who knew that you had to communicate about things that mattered to you openly and honestly, even when it was uncomfortable? And who knew that the baggage of the past would take any opportunity it could to rear its ugly head in any way it could? It did.

I couldn't see it then through my anxiety and misery, but God was working with a heavy hand on that island, ready and waiting for me to come to Him. He was working to rebuild my heart and my identity, as I furiously worked to build a home and bring order out of disorder.

God was working to rebuild my heart and my identity, as I furiously worked to build a home and bring order out of disorder.

+ Solid wood vintage
  furniture pieces
+ Solid brass decor
+ Vintage lighting
+ Vintage or antique
  hardware
+ Ceramics
+ Handmade, glazed
  clay bowls and
  containers
+ Unique vintage
  frames
+ Vintage art
+ Books
+ Records

All of these items can
help bring a lived-in
and unique feel to any
home and are some of
my faves!

Furnishing an island home can be very, very expensive. The less pricey options tended to be very tropical, which has never been my style. So, being the resourceful girl that I am, I began shopping thrift stores for pieces I liked that others might overlook. You know the ones, right? A scratched and faded dresser with good lines or a banged-up armoire missing some hardware and sitting catawampus in the corner of a shop. I knew that if I could pay a good price for them, I could turn them into pieces of beauty once again. And that's exactly what I did.

Every piece of furniture I found and painted became another brick in the foundation of God's healing and restorative power in my life. When I arrived in Hawaii, I was a die-hard perfectionist—more focused on the appearance of joy and contentment than actually being joyful or content. I expected others to make me happy and that pretty things could fill any chinks in my armor. But God knew better, of course, and set out to show me that I couldn't go on like that anymore.

> Every piece of furniture I found and painted became another brick in the foundation of God's healing and restorative power in my life.

In this He offered visions of what life could be like without my holding on to the lie that I wasn't good enough. He showed me the harsh reality

RESTORE, REDO, REFINISH

If you're intimidated by just the idea of restoring furniture, don't sweat it. You don't have to stir up your inner Joanna Gaines to get started, and your final product doesn't have to be museum quality. Just follow a few simple steps, and be confident that no matter what you end up with, you'll have a memento of the love you're putting into your home. (And if you really don't like the result, you can always "flip it" and sell it online!) The more you do this kind of thing, the better you'll get.

Where to begin?

So you've pinpointed a piece in the secondhand shop that strikes your fancy. Should you stain it? Wax it? Oil? Paint? Whether it's a fine piece of furniture or a banged-up piece begging for a revival, deciding what to do with an item once you find it can be pretty intimidating. Nine times out of ten, if you're grabbing your next favorite item from the thrift store, you're going to begin by stripping and sanding. It wasn't often that I found projects that were in perfect condition. When I did, I considered myself pretty lucky, but also bummed because the restoration process is such a blast!

Here's how you start:

1 **Find a sturdy piece of furniture.** Look for good bones, preferably solid wood with no loose joints.

2 **Research.** You may want to watch a video or two online of people refinishing a piece like yours, or talk to someone at your local hardware store to get advice and an idea of what's possible. These basic steps will get you started.

3   **Take your find to a covered, well-ventilated area.** Think: a carport, garage, or room with good windows and airflow. Make it as dust-free as possible with a vacuum and a mop.

4   **Clean your piece before you begin any work on it.** You will want to be sure that your piece is clean before you begin any work on it. You can purchase cleaners especially designed for this or you can make your own solution by diluting some dish soap in warm water. If you choose to go the premade route, be sure to follow the directions on the package and use gloves to keep those beautiful hands of yours looking lovely. For dressers or pieces with drawers, this will involve pulling out all drawers and cleaning behind them. In older pieces, you may even find a few treasures! I like using old paintbrushes that have been retired to clean in the cracks of pieces. You can also use a wet-dry vacuum as well to grab hold of the grub that you find. Just be prepared to get a little dirty during this process. It's often not pretty, but so worth it. Use an old towel for this and let air dry—then you can see what needs to be sanded or stripped. (Don't sand wet wood.)

5   **Once it's dry, sand or use chemical stripper to remove the old finish.** Don't use a belt sander until you know if the wood is veneer or solid! Make sure never to use chemical stripper in your living space unless it's fume free.

6   **Prepare the surface.** Fill dings with putty or wood filler. For paint, use a primer. I used chalk paint often when refinishing because I loved that there wasn't much of a need for primer with it. This means time saved, which means more time to do more pieces. For stain, research oil or other products to restore the surface and help the finish go on smooth.

7 **Apply your finish according to instructions.** Use as many coats as you need. I typically ran two to three coats once the foundation of the piece had been restored and it was ready for its new look.

8 **Once it's dry, wipe it down or buff** with furniture wax (for chalk paint) or a topcoat to give it a smooth, clean finish and to protect it for years to come.

of placing value in our home and possessions. He shifted my perspective and showed me that the expectations that I'd had for years were not set by Him but had been set in place based on my own home experiences, broken relationships, and unmet emotional needs. God reveals to heal. And that's just what He did.

It wasn't easy. To the contrary, it was a painful journey, but, as crazy as it may sound, in the best way. God was with me all the way. As I look back on this time, I can't imagine walking through it without Him walking right alongside me. He had taken me far away from anyone with any expectations about me. There was nothing for me to live up to anymore—no one with any preconceived notions of who I *should* be. There was only Him, waiting to show me all the wonderful things I *could* be.

A DEEPER RESTORATION

It might sound strange that restoring furniture led to God restoring me, but that's what happened. He showed me that I have a gift for making things beautiful, and He used that gift to help me find His peace, His joy, and my identity in Him through the stripping down, sanding, painting, and decorative detailing techniques. He used the gift He'd placed in me to heal my faded, cracked, and banged-up heart. Stripping off those layers of paint from the furniture, I felt the layers of pain and bumps and bruises being sanded away. I felt a new kind of freedom. It was as though for years someone had been holding their hand over my face, preventing full breathing, then all of a sudden, the hand lifted, and I could take in full breaths again.

Even now, as I think back, I am freshly amazed at how relentlessly

Restoring
furniture led
to God
restoring me.

pursued I was by Him. God stripped away my defense mechanisms, my coping techniques, all the things I used to hide my true self from everyone around me. While I was working with my hands, He led my mind down to the intimate details of my life and forced me to confront why I was the way I was, to deal with the grief of my past and let Him wash it away with my tears. He reminded me that He's not a superficial God. He didn't just want the perfect outward shell I was presenting to everyone; He wanted all of me—even the far-from-perfect, wounded, small part. But in order for Him to get to my heart and make me what He intended, I needed to have some things stripped away. Hawaii was the only place I'd lived where that could happen because everything that I'd used to make myself comfortable or to make myself believe I was living a full life was gone.

I'm constantly amazed at the method that God used to restore me. He led me to items others deemed unnecessary, without purpose, and helped me "breathe" life into them again. He was giving me the creativity, the energy, and the desire to restore. With every stroke of the brush, there was a newfound freedom to create, to commune, and to commit to Him, as never before. I lived for my toddlers' midday naps and early bedtimes just so I could meet with Him once again. I needed it as much as the air I breathed. It revived and invigorated me in a way I'd never experienced. I met with God daily and on a more personal level than ever before.

In the midst of kids running around our home, when the dishes and loads of laundry piled high, I found times of solitude and peace. I'd found my place. I found home in Him, and it was exhilarating. Of course, at the time, I never realized that was what was happening. But life felt a bit lighter and my heavy loads felt lifted. For the first time in a long time, I began to see my life, and my place in it, in a whole new way.

An exchange happened there in my dusty garage, filled with tools and paint fumes. God showed me, through the things I'd taken for granted in life, like my kids and the community He'd given us. He reminded me that freedom is only found by living in Him. And when I choose to give myself to Him in a real way, I am truly free to express the creative gifts and talents stored deep down inside me. But God never intended for me to use my gifts only on furniture; He showed me what real restoration in

REFLECT

- What kinds of things in the home do you fixate on that help you feel safe, together, or in control? What stands in for your "identity"? For me it was perfect decor. For you it might be cleanliness, a full fridge and pantry, or something else. Why do you think that is?
- What are you really longing for when you desire these things? Write out a prayer you can pray as you encounter them, asking God to redeem them and restore your identity in Him.
- What kinds of things do you want God to "strip away" from your life? Your home? What would you pray that He'd replace them with?
- If you were moving to a completely new home, taking only what you loved, what items would you take with you, and what would you leave behind? Make a list, and try to offload a few of those unnecessary items through donating or reselling.

Him looked like so that I could help others find the same thing. For the first time in my life, I felt I knew what God was calling me to do, and it was exciting.

Friends, before we can begin to fill our homes with all the good things we can see, we need God to come in and sweep us off our feet. We need Him to remind us of who we are and that our value isn't found in the good things, but in the *good Him*. We want our homes to welcome those who enter into a space that doesn't just appeal to our visual senses but to the soul—that speaks of where we are in just about any season of life we may be walking through. This is a home that only God can offer, and it's one that you can only offer through a restorative relationship with Him.

I am completely convinced that God can use what's going on in our homes to restore our hearts. And I'm convinced that any urge you feel

A LITTLE DEEPER | HOME + SOUL

God, I know You have some renovation work to do on my heart, and I long to find out what that will be. Please take my drive to make a beautiful home on this earth and expand it into a longing for Your restoration of my identity—of one who is loved, secure, rescued, and restored through Jesus' work. Show me where I've been depending on external things to fill me up, and come with healing into those places. As I make the home You've given me more reflective of Your love, Your beauty, and Your care for our souls, please let me feel Your presence and guidance in ever-deepening ways. Amen.

to renew, refresh, and beautify your home—including the one that led you to pick up this book—reflects a deeper desire, and it's one that God longs to fulfill. He wants to restore your identity. You might not have an epiphany over paint cans like I did, but I know that as you approach the restoration of your home with God's restoration in mind, you'll end up with something much better than any picture in any magazine: a home with heart that's uniquely yours.

God can use what's going on in our homes to restore our hearts.

TOOLS OF THE TRADE

Let's talk some must-haves for anyone starting out restoring furniture. Here are a few tools to get you going:

+ SANDER | I remember my first sander. I felt so accomplished and like such a powerful woman when I purchased mine. While it's convenient to research online, nothing really beats walking into a brick-and-mortar shop, talking to pros, and putting your hands on the things you need. Then you can get an idea of the right tool for your particular project. These tend to take a beating, so products with warranties and long-lasting reputations will serve you well.

+ PLASTIC BAGS | I mean used grocery bags. These always come in handy for covering brushes when you need to stop in the middle of a job to go and cook dinner or nurse a little one, or just walk away because of life. You can't leave them on for weeks at a time, of course, but these work well for up to a couple of days and are a great alternative to the covers that some of your local hardware stores sell. No need to spend your money on those. Just place the bag over the brush and secure with a rubber band or twist tightly to seal.

+ DROP CLOTHS | Whether plastic or reusable cloths, you will want to have a stock of these to layer underneath whatever you are refinishing even if you're working in an outdoor studio. These will keep the mess contained.

+ PIECES OF FABRIC | When I first started redoing furniture, some of my favorite projects were upholstered pieces. Dining chairs and stools were particularly fun because of how easy they were to complete. But after doing this for a while, one of the best decisions I ever made was to disavow my need to be a "Jane of all trades." When it comes to upholstery, depending on your own skill level, let the pros handle the more complicated jobs. I began to see myself as more a curator or procurer, passing a piece and my fabric on to my passionate team to add their own talent and skill. It's a great way to build community too.

+ TEXTILES | Don't be afraid to use unconventional or unexpected fabrics for your reupholstery projects. Stepping outside the thrift store box, online shops like Etsy, your local antique shops, or even garage sales are great places to stock up. When doing so, buy those textiles that capture your heart and attention when you see them so you'll have them on hand when that perfect chair or sofa comes your way.

+ SIDE NOTE | No hoarding! If you've had them in your stash for longer than one year, chances are, you're not going to use them. Pass them along. I like to keep my finds neatly stored in what I call my styling closet. When I am not using them for reupholstery projects, they can also come in handy for styling or decor projects around the house, photo shoots, or even tablecloths or runners.

CHAPTER 2

MY HOME STORY

Yet this I call to mind
and therefore I have hope:
Because of the LORD's great love we are not consumed,
for his compassions never fail.
They are new every morning;
great is your faithfulness.

–LAMENTATIONS 3:21–23

Beyond throw cushions and candle holders, our *stories* make our homes what they are, and inform what we want home to be. Embracing our stories will leave us with something deeper, richer, stronger than mere decoration. It will help us build a home that's true to us—one of a kind. So to get us there, let me begin by telling you my home story.

Home for me, growing up, wasn't always a place of rest or restoration. Everyone in my family loved me *very* much and wanted what was best for me, but, as I mentioned, that didn't necessarily translate into a home where I always felt accepted or free to be myself. I came up with ways to manage the chaos and often dreamt of that safe, free place I would one day build with my own family. I had no idea at the time how much my story would influence my sense of home for years to come—from my motivations to every small decision I made.

Like many kids, I grew up without a father. My mother and I lived with my grandparents, surrounded by aunts and cousins. My grandfather passed away when I was six years old, leaving us all without any sort of male presence. It was all girls, all the time.

These women shaped and molded me into the woman I am today—no doubt. They taught me to be strong, persistent, and inventive, and I am so grateful for them. But I'd be remiss to say that being raised by a single parent doesn't come with negatives.

Not having my grandfather in the home left quite a hole in our family or at least in my heart, but my mom, it seemed to me, took it the hardest. She had weathered more than her fair share of heartbreak and grief already, and she struggled with depression on and off for as long as I can remember. She suffered from a few mental breakdowns throughout my formative school years and was gone for periods of time while receiving help. She left me with a house full of amazing women who cared deeply for me, but no one could replace my mom, whom I desperately needed at that time in my life.

My grandmother loved me well and did the heavy lifting of raising me. She never complained, and I know how lucky I was to have her, but she couldn't be mother and father and grandparents all rolled into one—no one could. This meant that some of the things I needed most were sometimes, albeit unintentionally, overlooked. I missed my grandfather, and I was confused and angered by my mother's absences. I felt lonely and like a bother. I found ways to remedy those feelings of loss and emptiness—I'd be perfect, for starters.

Nothing ever rang so true for me than my need to see goodness and beauty in the world around me, even if that meant crafting it myself. This idea, unfortunately, pushed the God who created me for wholeness further and further away from my heart.

> Nothing ever rang so true for me than my need to see goodness and beauty in the world around me, even if that meant crafting it myself.

Sure, everything was fine on the outside. Life went on. I was well behaved, popular, an accomplished student on the honor roll pretty often, and, for the most part, everyone thought I was happy. But internally, I longed unknowingly for the *Great Perfecter*—the One who would come and make everything right for real.

A HOME IDENTITY CRISIS

I carried that baggage with me into my first home when my husband and I got married at the end of college. I think a lot of us come into our

homes as adults with a bit of a home identity crisis. Our concepts of home are tied closely to how we grew up. What our parents did or didn't do in their homes informs what we think we should do or shouldn't do.

That's my story. I took all the things I liked about the home I grew up in and translated them quite robotically into what I thought my own home should look like. I did a darn good job at just that—making it *look* good—but it was all on the surface. I wasn't creating a place that nourished my soul or healed my bruised heart, even if it did look cute in pictures. I didn't even realize that some of what I was doing was hurting me more.

I became addicted to attaining a level of notoriety within the style and design community, which left me feeling even more empty and out of touch not only with my own life but, more importantly, with the people *in* it. If you've ever done anything for the sake of a pat on the back or a compliment, you'll know the dark place I was in at the time. The scary part is that I didn't even know I was in that pit until much later. Because of the grace and mercy of God, He reveals things in time and provides rescue and healing and respite to our hearts just when we need it. This was the case for me.

———

My first home with Larry was beyond humble—it was meager. But it was ours. It was the first place we landed together and the first place in which we began to dream of what our future lives and homes would be. Admittedly, I probably thought of home more than my hubby. He loves to see me in my element, but perfectly coordinated textiles and complementary rugs don't really get him going in the morning.

I recall dreaming a lot. I could see in my mind's eye the floor plan I wanted, with polished wood floors, tons of light, and a big chef's kitchen. I wanted a place that didn't just *look* good but that felt good—and that, at the end of the day, really *was* good, you know? Not just some superficial shell of a space that we just *called* home. I dreamed about bringing home our first baby, hosting Thanksgiving and Christmas, inviting friends over for game nights and long talks over coffee curled up by the fireplace.

I wanted our home to be warm and welcoming—a place we could live open lives with abandon. What I didn't want is a home that felt cold or stuffy. There's nothing more unwelcoming than a home that feels like a museum, where you're afraid to sit or touch anything. That was the opposite of what I wanted people to feel when they visited us or came to gather around our table.

> I wanted our home to be warm and welcoming—a place we could live open lives with abandon.

As I sat in that roach-infested studio apartment, I remember thinking, *This is not at all the house that I've dreamt of.* That grungy little apartment could not have been further from a reflection of who we were and the life we both wanted to create for ourselves. It was discouraging. I spent a lot of time comparing our beginnings with what it had taken

GOOD THINGS IN SMALL SPACES

You might be living in a home that doesn't perfectly reflect the story you want to be telling, and for a lot of us that's chalked up to a space issue. Years of rental-dwelling has taught me that you don't have to gut the place and renovate to achieve more of what you're going for. You can make it feel like home regardless of the amount of square footage you have to work with.

1 **Edit your stuff.** First, let's change our perspective about this idea that small equals bad. Instead of seeing it as a problem, let's see it as an opportunity to be a little more creative in our spaces. If you've got low ceilings or small spaces, pay attention to how much you fill your space with *stuff* and the arrangement of that stuff. Minimalism is all the rage these days, and while this may not be your favorite style, choosing to edit your personal items and decorative pieces will help smaller spaces feel less crowded and more clean and open. This is the goal with any room that is a bit space deficient.

2 **Use color.** Another way to make a small space feel large is selecting paint colors for your walls, specifically your living spaces, that open up the space instead of closing it off. White is always a win but sometimes not the most ideal. If white just isn't an option for you, consider painting your ceiling an alternative or contrasting color to offer the illusion of tall ceilings, or selecting flooring that is lighter in color.

3 **Use textiles.** Hanging curtains not only brings personality and warmth to a space, but if you're dealing with low ceilings in a small

space, they can also create the illusion of higher ceilings in a room. The general rule for this is that the rod should sit four to six inches above the top of your window. If you have trim work, the rod should hang four to six inches above the trim. Hang your curtains high. The idea is to do whatever you can in a smaller space to draw the eye up and add some drama. Choosing panels isn't easy. Trust me, I know. Challenge yourself to step out of the box by finding some patterns that complement the rest of your room. It's visual candy for everyone and also pulls the eye and mind away from the fact that your space may feel a bit cramped.

4   **Strategize with furniture.** Furniture can be the foundation for everything else in a space. To use your furniture appropriately in your space, you will want to take inventory of what you have. Much like the games we help our eyes play with textiles, more substantial furniture in a small room gives the illusion that a space is much larger than it actually is. Now, I'm not saying to fill your space with large-scale pieces. This will only congest your space and make it feel less cozy. But when selecting pieces like sofas, lounge chairs, and the like, consider the scale of your room versus the scale of your furniture. While proportion is very important, function is equally as important. Find pieces that perform double duty: sofas that turn into beds or side tables that nest. Mount your television instead of using a media stand, and use the space underneath for storage or for extra seating. It's fun to think nontraditionally, and you'll be surprised at what you come up with to create a space that is both functional and fun.

other people and designers years to build and create. I wasn't content. I was grumpy and childish. I don't think I ever complained out loud, but inside my head, the war raged. It was all too common for me to rehearse comments like "I wish I had . . ." or "This isn't like so and so's," until they became a toxic anthem that would surely become the death of any hopes, dreams, and desires if I wasn't careful.

While I understood how damaging and reckless this kind of self-talk could be, for some reason, I just could not stop it. I wanted bigger and better right away. I thought having the perfect house would make me a perfect wife, a perfect friend—a perfect person. I didn't understand then that all the beautiful light, fancy fixtures, and hardwood floors in the world wouldn't make my home and my life automatically open, restorative, and peaceful. God taught me that lesson little by little in every home we rented—in every imperfect dwelling we made the best of. Slowly but surely I came to realize that to create spaces that were regenerative in every way, I first had to be regenerated. I first had to have a heart made whole.

EXPECTATIONS

I'm an only child. For most of my life I'd say I pretty much got whatever I wanted whenever I wanted it from the time I was born. (Most of my aunts and my uncle can vouch for that.) There wasn't anything that my grandparents, my papaw and memaw, wouldn't do to make me happy, it seemed. They spoiled me because they loved me, but it bred in me a heart that never knew how to be content without having the things I wanted.

This was something I never had to face until I married my husband. (You can all say a little prayer for my Larry.) I went through so many

I thought having the perfect house would make a perfect wife, a perfect friend—a perfect person.

SMALL CHANGES, BIG IMPACT

Make an impact without breaking the bank or putting in a lot of work.

1 **Removable Wallpaper** | This is one of my favorite ways to bring color, pattern, and personality to a space, especially smaller spaces like bathrooms and even closets.

2 **Rugs** | Rugs are an easy way to change the entire feel of a space. I love finding vintage ones at thrift shops (if you find one you love, opt for having it professionally cleaned before using it in your home, no matter the condition). But I also love scouring the internet to find brands that source them at a low cost to the public.

3 **Curtains** | You don't need high-end customs to make a big impact with curtains. There are many companies that offer higher quality products at a lower cost. A quick search online should provide some guidance and offerings for you. If you're handy with a sewing machine, choose to DIY. This opens up a world of possibilities as you have the option of shopping your local fabric stores for what you believe best fits the style and look of the space you are placing them in.

4 **Flowers + Plants** | Plants are also one of my favorite ways to impact a space. They bring life to just about any space—even bathrooms— and provide direction for the eyes to travel in a room as well as adding texture.

5 **Paint** | If this were a "101" class, I'm pretty sure this would be the first topic discussed. This basic tool of the trade is not only a no-nonsense way of defining spaces but also has the ability to bring freshness and an entirely new look to any room. It's an oldie but a goodie.

seasons of expecting to be *made* happy, and this especially reared its ugly head in the area of our home. If a beautiful home meant I was successful and doing a great job as a wife and mother, well then, I was going to make my home beautiful. I didn't want out-of-date decor and hand-me-down, not-my-style furniture. I wanted new and shiny and beautiful. And the ultimate fulfillment of that, in my mind, would be a home of our own.

I won't say that this little monster doesn't rear its ugly head every now and then, but now I can own up to and recognize it as an unhealthy thought pattern. Some of that freedom came with age and realizing what's actually important. Life has a funny way of teaching us things like that from time to time. I have also seen the destruction that comes from believing that the world is owed to me, that *things* make me happy, and that it is everyone's job but my own to carry my joy like the treasure it actually is.

Ten years into our marriage something pretty significant happened. We decided to separate from the military and live a civilian life. Larry had been in the military since we'd gotten married, so we'd never actually lived a "normal" life. We left the base in Hawaii and moved back to Seattle, where we'd been stationed briefly before. We packed up everything we owned and moved into a rental. Again.

I was less than pleased. I wanted a real home. A permanent home. A home we owned. After over a decade of bouncing from rental to rental and base to base, I wanted something that could be ours. I told myself that it was only temporary and that we would find a home to call our own sooner rather than later.

+ AREA RUGS | They
help define small
spaces and can be
an inexpensive win.

+ A SPACE TO
CALL YOUR
OWN | Whether
it's a corner in
your bedroom or
living room, find a
space that you can
dedicate to reading
your favorite book,
listening to your
favorite audiobook,
or staring out the
window. This will
help your temporary
dwelling feel more
like a permanent
home.

Well, later turned into *much* later—and after three years in that rental we had to move to yet another rental. I was so discouraged. But I decided that instead of running away from my emotions or stuffing them, I'd lean in to God and what I felt He was offering me: an opportunity to gain new perspective on His direction in our lives.

Those parts of my heart that had longed for more, longed for an amazing gourmet kitchen with designer fixtures and furniture, those parts of my heart that compared my home to others' and what others had, those voices that whispered a need for perfection began to dissipate, and I began to experience a peace that I'd never felt before. I was no longer trying to ease the pain of my story with external things; instead, God was redeeming that story, taking me from desperation to contentment, and exposing and healing wounds I would just as soon have papered over or hidden beneath piles of perfect cushions. This was a process—and still is—of trusting God and hearing His voice. It's a trading of what I wanted and may have believed to be important (the idea of a perfect home that tended all my wounds) for the purpose our lives are actually meant to fulfill with Him—our new story.

LEARNING CONTENTEDNESS

So what turned the tide? How did God lead me out of the old story and into the new? It all started with gratitude. Sometimes when you pray for something so long, you don't even realize that you're praying anymore. I like to call these "prayers of the heart." Mine was this: *Lord, help me be grateful. Thankful. Help me see the life You have given us through Your eyes and not my own. Help me seek Your plans in all of this.* In the midst of that move to Seattle, He answered.

I believe God wants our desires to line up with His. He desires that we desire Him above all things, focus on Him, and lean in to Him. The apostle Paul said it perfectly:

Actually, I don't have a sense of needing anything personally. I've learned by now to be quite content whatever my circumstances. I'm just as happy with little as with much, with much as with little. I've found the recipe for being happy whether full or hungry, hands full or hands empty. Whatever I have, wherever I am, I can make it through anything in the One who makes me who I am. (Philippians 4:12 MSG)

This verse fits like a glove. No matter where we are in life, no matter where life takes us, or whether we have enough, more than enough, or a lack, we can be confident. We can be happy and trust the One who has created us. We can trust Him with the houses we live in and the means to make those houses homes. We can trust Him with it all.

If we take another look at that passage, Paul said that he "learned" this attitude of grateful confidence. But the truth is that most of us are still learning. Most of us struggle with living out our stories on a daily basis. So, what do you do in the waiting? What do you do when the odds seem stacked against you and you just don't know how to move forward?

To learn how to be content, have a more fulfilled life, and actually hear God in our lives and in our homes, we must lean in to our stories and embrace gratefulness within them.

This is something that doesn't come naturally for most of us. Whether you're like me and have been honing this skill of creating a healing home your entire life, or life has left you feeling empty and

+ LIGHTING | This has been key for us in the past. Changing out lighting adds a custom feel and, thus, will give your space a more personal touch.

+ REMOVABLE WALLPAPER | Most renters won't allow for traditional wallpaper, but these days there are so many options for temporary wall coverings. This, again, helps a temporary space feel much more personal and is one that reflects your personality as the renter.

We can trust Him with the houses
we live in and the means to make those
houses homes. We can trust Him with it all.

unfulfilled, our landing space is ultimately the same—we begin to fill our lives with *things* instead of what really matters.

Now, in no way am I saying that the things we put in our homes don't matter. What I *am* saying is that we have to learn to put them in their proper place—that is, in the service of our new story, and of those God has given us to live and do life with. As we walk forward together, I hope you'll look at your own story with new eyes—unflinchingly, embracing the beauty that comes from even the things you would rather forget. Your story is still happening, and you can approach setting the stage for it to play out with an open heart.

REFLECT

- How would you describe your home story? How was your idea of the home you wanted informed by your upbringing, both positively and negatively?
- Are there any ways in which this idea is at odds with reality? What could God be teaching you in that space of disconnect?
- What kind of story do you want your home to tell? How can gratefulness play a key part in that story?

A LITTLE DEEPER | HOME + SOUL

God, please lead me into the new story You are writing for my life. Show me how to embrace it, and give me wisdom and discernment as I set the stage in my home for that story. Please tenderly care for my past hurts, opening my eyes to the ways they affect my motivations and decisions. Redeem this story, and help me embrace it fully.

FLOOR RESCUE

Our floors have run the gamut in each and every home we've lived in. They've mostly been terrible, with the exception of our home in Hawaii. Those floors were stunning. I still dream of them from time to time. If you're like me and are a fan of rugs (even if you aren't, I promise, I'll win you over), you can't pass up an opportunity to bring home a beautiful rug. Vintage ones are my favorite. When they're not too worn, they offer an immediate sense of comfort and home and add character to a once cold space.

If you're tempted to stay away from rugs because you don't know how to choose the appropriate size for your space, have no fear. If your goal is to pull a space together while also covering floors that aren't eye candy, go a bit larger when choosing yours. It's always better to go a little larger than you're comfortable with. Nothing makes a room feel more awkward than a tiny rug that's ill-fit for the space. I love layering rugs as well. When layering, just remember to choose a neutral base, like a jute rug or something solid or plain. This way, no matter how your style or taste may change, the rug you choose to throw over your foundation rug will look good with it.

YOUR WISH LIST | THE ELEMENTS OF YOUR STORY

If you're reading a book like this, chances are you have a wish list of things you'd like to do to or add to your home. Maybe it's a certain kind of seating area, storage solutions, or the makings of a gallery wall. Whatever your top five wishes are for your home, write them down below. Then next to them write the internal goal: the home story you hope to use these pieces to tell. Ask God to use this to clarify your wants and needs, and to help you embrace the story He's telling now in your life.

Examples:

L-SHAPED SECTIONAL → A comfy place to crash and escape from busy life. Space for friends to take a load off, feel comfortable snuggling under throws, or sip coffee together.

God, I want my home story to include a place of retreat and comfort for me and for friends. Help me put that warmth and community first, trusting that You'll provide a way, with or without the items on my wish list.

HALLWAY STORAGE BUILT-INS → A place to hide coats, recycling, bags, and utility gear. A calm and organized entrance to our home.

God, please keep our stuff from overwhelming us and those who enter our home. I want my home story to include a brave fight against chaos. Please show us how to wrangle our things and put them in their right place—but to remember that this is less important than the warmth with which we welcome people in.

Fill in your wishes, motivations, and prayers below:

_____

_____

_____

_____

_____

_____

_____

_____

_____

CHAPTER 3

THE FREE HOME

Where the Spirit of the Lord is, there is freedom.

—2 CORINTHIANS 3:17

So, what was your story? Do you know a little more about who you are and how you got there? Even more, do you know what makes your heart beat with passion and invigorates you? What gives you life and breath? Okay, okay, I know. Those are deep questions and I kind of went there pretty quickly, but it's important to wrestle with them for ourselves and our homes.

Typically, when we feel less *at* home, it's because we have a problem *embracing* who we are, our stories, and how that connects us in our homes. Now that you've thought a little more about your story, it's time to explore more about how that directly relates to your living space today—in the present. Maybe you aren't happy with your house or apartment itself—you hate the drafty windows or the peeling linoleum floors or the hideously ugly, old wallpaper. It doesn't feel like a place where you belong. But even if your current place is far from where you want it to be, I want to encourage you to *own it*.

This time in this space is part of your story. It can be a part where you pout and sulk and make yourself and everyone around you miserable with your dissatisfied heart, or it can be a part where you lean in to God and let His restoration flow through you to your space.

This time in this space is part of your story.

At this point, you're probably wondering where all the practical points for restoring joy in your home are. How can you lean in if all you feel like doing is pouting, complaining, and retreating? If this is you, I promise, you will get there. I do believe, however, that before we can have joy in the spaces we live in, we have to know what steals the joy we have in the first place.

BREAK FREE FROM COMPARISON

For me, and I am sure many of you out there will relate, social media is one of my biggest "joy suckers." While it's a tool that I use almost daily to connect with distant family and friends and even some of you, I'm still

1. Begin with a base.
You will want to
choose three or
four items to do so.
For this example,
we will use a tray,
a container of your
choice, and some
type of coffee table
book that will add
a pop of color or
pattern to the table.

2. Add height. This is
where you will want to
add a vase with florals
or greenery, more
books to stack, and
perhaps even more
decorative items that
offer varying height.

3. Accessorize. These are
items that add finishing
touches and make the
tabletop feel more
complete. Consider

human. Every now and then I have to remind myself that the freedom I seek in my home can sometimes be sabotaged when I compare or become complacent with where I am or how I live.

The lie that most of us choose to believe is that there is one right way to be. We believe that we should look to others to make sure we're on the right track, that our homes and lives should be like theirs. Where's the fun in that?

> # The lie that most of us believe is that there is one right way to be.

It's far too easy in this day and age to just go online and compare, compare, compare. We've all been there, right? There you are, reading a blog, looking through an article, or perusing at your favorite designer's Instagram feed, and it hits you: *I wish my home looked like that. I wish I could afford to remodel my kitchen. Why do her cabinets look like that? Why doesn't our family do things like that together? I wish my husband would sweep me off my feet like that.* Before you know it, you've been sucked into a vortex of comparing your life, your family, and your home to those of people you don't even know, and you feel anything but peaceful or joyful. How can you break free?

Second Corinthians 3:17–18 says, "The Lord is the Spirit, and where the Spirit of the Lord is, there is freedom. And we all, with unveiled face, beholding the glory of the Lord, are being transformed into the same image from one degree of glory to another. For this comes from the Lord who is the Spirit" (ESV).

There is freedom. I love that phrase. Now, *freedom* isn't a word you hear often in relation to home, but it's one that is just as important as *sofa* or *lamp*.

Freedom comes in allowing God to work in hearts and lives through your gifts, your home, and the relationships you nurture there. There is freedom in embracing imperfections and admitting that you don't fit into cultural boxes, and that you're just uniquely you, walking out the ever-evolving journey God has called you to walk in confidence with Him. So invite Him in. When you feel the pull toward comparison, put down the phone, shut the computer, turn off the TV, close the book, and ask again for the freedom that is yours. Be aware of the things that stifle the freedom to embrace *your* unique story in your home, and don't let comparison crush the instincts God gave you. You can turn it around by going back to the Source of your soul, making room for Him in your circumstances. There's freedom there.

BREAK FREE FROM SELF-DOUBT AND CREATIVE DROUGHT

I'm not saying to avoid TV, magazines, or social media altogether. They all have their place—keeping up with people, finding inspiration, learning about the things others are doing that you might want to try, and even a gathering in a digital way as you reach out and really connect online. But we run the risk of damaging our hard-won creative spirits when we lean too much on others and choose not to trust God, ourselves, and our own creative gifts.

adding items that give it more of a personal touch like small picture frames showcasing family photos or pets or favorite items collected from vacations.

PRAY THROUGH COMPARISON

Here are some short prayers to help you appreciate others' spaces, pictures, and posts without falling into the trap of comparison. The next time you feel it rise, invite God in with these comparison busters:

+ GRATITUDE | *Thank You for blessing this person with [that enviable thing]. Please be glorified in his or her life. Thank You for what You've given uniquely to me too.*

+ INSPIRATION | *God, please purify my thoughts, straining out the envy and leaving only inspiration to work within my story. Show me how to never make more of something than it really is.*

+ UNPLUGGING | *Lord, give me discernment in what I allow into the mind-space You've given me. I want to honor You; show me when I'm heading the wrong way and need to change direction.*

We run the risk of damaging our hard-won creative spirits when we lean too much on others and choose not to trust God, ourselves, and our own creative gifts.

And for anyone who decided to tune me out after reading "creative gifts," I promise you're creative, and I promise you're gifted in your own unique way. Each of us was created by a creative God, who not only planted something in us but who, daily, sees and calls that something *out* in us. Whether we feel it or not, it's there. And this gift that each of us carries is unique to us as individuals. It's what makes us and our abilities so special.

If you've ever thought, *I just can't do this, I could never make a home as nice as that person's,* or *I'm not creative, together, or with-it enough,* I want you to back right out of that thought pattern. Our thoughts define us. Typically, what we think, we do. And what we do matters.

If you think poorly of yourself, that will create an atmosphere of unrest in your home. This has quite a trickle-down effect on your energy level, your home, and the resources you have to pour into others. How do I know? Well, I've been there too many times. God, in His grace, has reeled me in with His love and His kindness more times than I can count in relation to this feeling of insecurity in my own home.

Remember, God made you. He doesn't make mistakes. He created

No one else can do
what you can do in or
out of your home.

you lovingly and bestowed His gifts on you and in your heart. No one else can do what you can do in or out of your home. The next time you are tempted to berate your decorating skills or get down on yourself, remember that you have the unique opportunity to own what He has placed in you.

SHOW WHO YOU ARE

When I'm scrolling through image after image and comparing my home to online perfection, it's so easy to lose my own voice in the competition, trends, and fear of rejection. It's easy to let insecurities win out, putting chains on me and limiting my freedom to create and work the way God wants me to. Let me remind you: you will never be able to focus on creating a space that is uniquely yours without possessing full knowledge of just how amazing you actually are. That knowledge can become a beautiful display of freedom, spread and shared with others, in your home and life.

> You will never be able to focus on creating a space that is uniquely yours without possessing full knowledge of just how amazing you actually are.

The truth is, we don't really know how to be anyone else. We can't express ourselves, fully, in any other way than the way we've been created to. It's really hard to think of what you want to do when you're thinking of how someone else would do it. Creating a home that restores is about making space for everyone, yourself included, to be completely themselves. To do that, you have to be listening to who you are, the you God made you to be, and expressing that honestly in your home.

One of my favorite movies is *Black Panther*. If you haven't seen it, do yourself the favor. (You can thank me later.) One line from the movie stuck with me; it comes when King T'Challa is in the fight for his life, and the only way for him to come through it successfully is to remember who he is. So in a moment of complete desperation but affirmation, his mother yells for him to show his true self. This moment took my breath away.

It made me think about how many times God's voice had called me to the very same thing. I thought of how many times I'd chosen not to show my real self out of fear of judgment or misunderstanding, and how many opportunities I had missed to not only reflect who I was but who God was *in* me. And at the end of the day, our homes are the one place we get to be *who* we are. It's a safe place where we are allowed to express our personalities, styles, and flavor and, most importantly, the heart of who we are as individuals and as families.

When we can truly embrace who we are and express it freely, we will arrive at a place like no other. This is the sweet spot that a restored home represents. This place is a space between fear and perfection. It's a space where God can take the gifts that He has placed in you and use them to reach the hearts of people in whatever way you are meant to influence.

When we can truly embrace who we are and express it freely, we will arrive at a place like no other. This is the sweet spot that a restored home represents.

This, friend, is the beautiful dance. It's the loving relationship that we have with our Creator to be free to live the lives that He has called us to live. We are then enabled by Him to live fully, humbly, and courageously without one single apology for who we are. When others enter our homes, we want them to sense and experience Him in a way that they never have before and one that they will long for well after their departure.

A LITTLE DEEPER | HOME + SOUL

God, thank You for making me unique and creative. Please show me how to nurture, feed, and grow the creative instincts You placed within me and use them in the context of my home. Show me how to expand those instincts to encompass the story I'm living in and the people I share my space with. When comparison strikes, show me how to take back control and draw closer to You instead. Come in with Your Spirit, and bring freedom to my mind and to my home.

REFLECT

Think back to your story. What places and spaces have left an impression on you, or made you feel at home, inspired, or comfortable just to be you—not necessarily the person you want to be, but the one you *are*? Jot down a profile of that place and pinpoint what exactly about it made you feel that way. It just might inspire you to re-create that feeling in your own space. For instance, a trip to the botanical gardens may have made you feel refreshed and hopeful, so botanical prints in vibrant colors against neutral backgrounds could reflect a lovely memory of that for you.

Why these places made me feel:

REFRESHED

HOPEFUL

RELAXED

COZY

ACCEPTED

CONNECTED WITH OTHERS

CREATIVE

CHAPTER 4

THE POWER TO DREAM AGAIN

*Faith is confidence in what we hope for and
assurance about what we do not see.*

–HEBREWS 11:1

We've done a lot of thinking so far about our stories. Whether they're chaotic, unsettled, works in progress, or even painful, they are our greatest resource for building a beautiful, meaningful, authentic home. Our stories drive us—toward God and toward the things we want for our safe spaces. One of the wonderful benefits of working to make your home a place of peace, joy, and restoration is that it restores you *and* your story! When your home is a sanctuary, you can rest and recharge and turn your thoughts inward to nurture your own soul.

Sometimes, though, after facing all of unsettled, uncontrollable life, it's almost impossible to have the hope and energy left to dream.

When your home is a sanctuary, you can rest and recharge and turn your thoughts inward to nurture your own soul.

Owning a home and putting down permanent roots somewhere has been a long, deeply held dream of mine. It didn't make sense for us to buy property when we knew we wouldn't be able to stay while we were in the military, but that didn't make me want it any less! As we went from rental to rental, base to base, I kept that dream cradled in my heart—nurturing it and adding to it with every stop. It was the dream that got me through hard seasons and bad apartments and helped me rein in my spending as we saved our pennies for the day we could make my dream a reality. I knew we'd have to start with something modest and that I wasn't going to get everything on my dream wish list. But I was looking forward to finding the worst house in a great neighborhood and putting my spin on it. I dreamed about our first home in Seattle so often and so fiercely that it almost felt like I could make it happen through sheer force of will.

When we landed in Seattle, I was eager to make that dream come true. My husband and I found a rental to start and began house hunting. I knew it might take us a while, but in the back of my mind I was expecting something like those shows where the couple sees three great houses, makes a choice, and moves right in.

It was not like that.

The housing market in Seattle is extremely competitive, and even the most modest houses are very, *very* expensive. So we saw a lot of houses. Two years came and went, and our lease was not renewed on our rental. Instead of moving into our own home, we moved into yet another rental.

I was crushed. And just like that, the dream that had inspired me for twelve years became something I couldn't bear to think about. I felt that loss keenly. Around that same time, my mother passed away. Grief layered over grief, and I felt lost in it. On top of all of it, Larry's job required long hours. He was exhausted by the time he made it home each day, and the stress and pressure took a toll on our relationship.

Never one to give up, I slowly made that rental into a home for us. I was doing the work of putting things away, arranging pillows, and placing furniture, but I wasn't inspired, and I wasn't dreaming. But here I saw, yet again, that when God is in the midst of something, when we seek Him out as part of the process of creating home, things seem to fall into alignment.

We had some of the greatest landlords we could ask for and ended up having a wonderful relationship with them for a while after we moved. They let me make small changes to the landscaping, change some paint colors, and make other small updates that I felt the home needed to make it feel more like ours, even though it was far from that in reality. I don't believe those good landlords were simply luck of the draw; I believe God used them to address my hurting heart and help me dream again.

MY FAVORITE RESTORATIVE PAINT COLORS | BEYOND BASIC WHITE

1. BEHR "IN THE MOMENT"
   + Why: peaceful + calm
   + Where: walls, kitchen cabinetry, furniture

2. BENJAMIN MOORE "METROPOLITAN"
   + Why: restful + cool
   + Where: walls, kitchen cabinetry

3. BEHR "SOFT FOCUS"
   + Why: calm + grounding
   + Where: walls (especially bedroom and bath)

REVIVE YOUR DREAMS

Have you ever had a dream that felt like it was just about to die, but then a little bit of life got breathed back into it unexpectedly? Is there a dream in your heart for your home that you've just about given up on? What would happen if you committed that dream to God and asked Him to do with it what He would? He might surprise you by sending inspiration in the smallest, most unexpected ways.

This is the power of dreaming with God, but it's also the power of identity in our homes. This is the power of collecting all our passions for our homes and what we hope they will be, giving them to God, and letting Him do what He does best—turn them into something bigger than anything we could ever imagine.

Restoration House is a testimony of just that. Even more, my life is a testimony of God being God and breathing life over and over again into our home and my dreams. They are His dreams, and they are fulfilled by His power.

What are your dreams? Your passions? What are your desires when it comes to your home or life in general? To be honest, it doesn't really matter how simple or insignificant they may be; they are important, and in the big scheme of things they ultimately matter to God. As I've shared, my story isn't perfect. Things in my life haven't always come together the way I wanted them to. But God is writing a bigger story. The things that are imperfect in our eyes become a beautiful fulfillment of His grace and His mercy.

When I changed my ideas about who I was and what *I* wanted my life to look like (perfect) versus what God would have my life truly be, I found the power to dream again. I found the power to collaborate with

God is writing a bigger story. The things that are imperfect in our eyes become a beautiful fulfillment of His grace and His mercy.

Him to make life the best it could be. This is where the sweet journey of embracing all my story entailed began.

———

We all have dreams for our homes and our lives. Making space for dreams to flourish helps us remember that our stories will continue. In ups and downs, we can trust that "the LORD works out everything to its proper end" (Proverbs 16:4). Our stories will change, grow, and be led by God. They'll be deeply shaped by the people He puts in our lives. And our homes will change and grow right along with them. As you begin to give your dreams over to God, He'll remind you to celebrate with Him over how far He has taken you already. In your home and in your heart, take Him up on that invitation.

REFLECT

- Are there any dreams for your home that have been stifled by circumstance? If so, how can you begin to give them to God?
- How can remembering your story help revive those dreams?
- In what small ways could God be encouraging you to keep those dreams alive?

A LITTLE DEEPER | HOME + SOUL

God, thank You for the unique identity and story You've given me. When at times I want to trade it for another, remind me how carefully You chose and made me, those in my family, and those with whom I share my home. Show me how to celebrate it in the home You've put me in; I want You to be at the center of that celebration. Lead me, guide me, inspire me, and remind me that my story with You has just begun.

WHAT'S YOUR STORY?

Think back on this journey so far. What's your story? What's your home story? The blending of that story is what makes your home, well, your home. When we let God into our home story, when He is an integral part of our identity in our homes, we'll notice a significant shift in the way we feel and, consequently, the way our homes feel to others.

Here are a few creative ways you can allow that story to unfold visually and tell the story of restoration over and over again in your own home.

1. **Letters of Gratitude** | Write out your home story. If kids or family live with you, have them do the same. Focus on times when you thought something would work out one way but, to your favor, it worked out another. This not only is a great way to remember where you've come from but also creates unique art to adorn the walls of your home.

2. **Repurpose, Repurpose, Repurpose** | Have you rebuilt a home or remodeled? Carried pieces from your childhood or heirlooms from a family member? Use them. Allow these pieces to tell the story of your home and your life on a bookshelf, in a frame, or on your walls. Don't be afraid to repurpose and convert items and use them in unintended ways:

+ An old pediment from a bed works wonders atop a slider door or window as an architectural accent. Repurpose is the name of the game when it comes to using vintage and antique items in your space.

+ Take an old wooden milk crate, add wheels, and top with a covered cushion for some mobile footstool fun in your space. If you have kiddos, this is a great option for a kids' table as it can also double as storage for knickknacks such as art tools and toys.

+ If you can get a hold of them, frame plans or architectural renderings from your childhood home or a place special to you to remind you of happy times.

+ Use old china and bowls for planters to create a wall full of unexpected art.

+ Repurpose old house numbers or hardware on bookshelves to add a bit of character, bring in texture, or add an architectural element to the space.

+ Cuttings from plants in frames are fun and an inexpensive way to give rooms a natural feel and create conversation. Perhaps you have a favorite tree at your family vacation destination. Grab a few leaves, press them, and frame them to give your botanical art a story to tell.

+ Working on a gallery wall can evoke all sorts of emotions. Try not to think too hard about what to include when creating a collection in your home. Whether you're hanging them on your walls or using a shelf, consider framing family photography and art in all shapes and sizes to create visual interest and keep the eyes moving around your space.

3 **Symbolic Storytelling** | If you were to think of your story as a book, how would you divide it into epochs, or time periods? Consider choosing an object to display that reminds you of the good times of each epoch. They don't have to actually *be* items from specific epochs, but they could remind you of what made your journey so special.

4 **A Sense of Place** | Get inspired by the history of the town you live in. Look for maps, old prints, local foliage, artisan crafts, and historic items that could help knit your home into the landscape of where you are. Consider doing this for places you've lived or loved, or places you dream of visiting one day.

PART 2

A RESTORED SPACE FOR YOU

My people will live in peaceful dwelling places,
in secure homes,
in undisturbed places of rest.

–ISAIAH 32:18

CHAPTER 5

A NEW NAME

Restore us to yourself, Lord, that we may return;
renew our days as of old.

—LAMENTATIONS 5:21

You might not know it, but a few years back, when I was still painting and restoring furniture, Restoration House had a different name—Me 'n' My House (MNMH). I know; so clever. (Total sarcasm.) A couple of years into my business, I felt that, because of what God had done in me through MNMH, it deserved a name change. Thus, *Restoration House* was born. It was nothing earth-shattering, but it is just as significant now as it was then because I've learned that there's power in a name.

I've learned that there's power in a name.

This scripture is one of my favorites:

[The Lord has sent me] to care for the needs of all who mourn in Zion, give them bouquets of roses instead of ashes, messages of joy instead of news of doom, a praising heart instead of a languid spirit. Rename them "Oaks of Righteousness" planted by God to display his glory. (Isaiah 61:3 MSG)

I want you to pay close attention to the part that talks about renaming. Let's think about what this means in relation to our homes.

If you picked up this book, it's because you want to create a home that restores you, your family, and your friends and community. What is your home lacking now to make that happen? Is your home hectic and unorganized and stressful? Outdated and filled with hand-me-downs you are sick to death of looking at? Neutral to the point of boredom because you can't decide what to do next? Take a few minutes to walk through your home with the freshest eyes you can muster. What would your home's name be right now? What would you like it to be? It may feel a bit silly, but push past that feeling. I promise it will be worth it.

Sometimes it can be difficult to look around and figure out where to start when it comes to decorating or redecorating your home, and it can be quite an intimidating process for even the most studied designer.

To make it a little easier on yourself and to start the process, begin by

telling yourself that it doesn't need to be perfect. If you're not a designer, that's okay. There's no pressure to be something you aren't, and the more you are able to release this idea, the easier it will become to think about how you want your home to *feel* when you and others walk in. Is the home of your heart a place of joy or peace? What will it bring to those who enter? Once you've determined those things, name your house. You don't need to shout this from the rooftops. It can be between you and God. But honestly, this will help you overcome the challenge of beginning to create a home that reflects the one you've dreamed of.

SPRUCE IT UP!

When shopping for paint colors for your walls, choose colors that are calm and peaceful and that naturally complement not only the mood you are trying to set for your home, but also the overall feel you've set as a goal. This way you have created a backdrop to add or remove color from as you please for future spruce-ups and restyling. I love to change things up one or two times a year, but repainting can be a lot of work. Instead I bring in new and fresh colors with accessories and art.

When shopping at thrift stores for furniture and accessories, look for quality solid wood pieces and pure metals, and don't dismiss something because it's covered in dust. There's pretty much nothing that a little soap, warm water, and elbow grease can't shine up like new. In fact, the grimier an item, the more likely you are to be able to get it for a good price!

Don't overlook the craft section of your favorite big box store for acrylic paints and smaller pieces to personalize, like unfinished picture frames and decor pieces. If painting isn't your thing, no worries. I personally love a natural wood side table or frame. If you find yourself always reaching for the paint brush, try something new and let your furniture go *au naturale*. This will also help to give your space a fresh and organic feel.

What's my home name? Well, of course it's *Restoration House*. It's a dream that I've long carried and that God continues to breathe into with each passing year. He can do the same for you.

What you decide for your home is completely up to you, but feel the freedom to be as practical or as abstract as you'd like. This will, no doubt, help when you begin to lay things out.

MAKE IT MATCH

Once you have an idea for a name, look around and determine three key things you can accomplish to get you closer to your ideal home. And, no, you can't list gutting the house and redoing it from the studs out! Set a reasonable budget for yourself, and look for things you can do within that budget. Paint is cheap as long as you are willing to paint yourself. You can experiment with the wide variety of hardware and tile offered at your local home and hardware stores. You can even find great furniture pieces at thrift stores for good prices and paint or refinish them yourself for a fresh look. It might seem like such small changes won't matter, but I promise you they will!

For example, I have a friend who bought a house that looked as though someone literally vomited a different paint color in *every single room*. It was exhausting even before she brought in her furniture. Now, this friend likes color and pattern, but it was too much even for her. The house needed other work too—it had hideous light fixtures, dinged-up floors, popcorn ceilings, outdated hardware, and a kitchen that was far from gourmet. She also needed furniture since the home was much bigger than her previous place. With a limited budget, she was overwhelmed. Instead of panicking or just ignoring the issues, she decided the floors, ceilings, and walls were her biggest obstacles. So she rolled up her sleeves and got to work. She spent hours scraping and sanding ceilings until they were popcorn free and smooth. Then she spent even more hours painting every inch of trim and ceiling bright white and the walls a moody gray. She finished it all up by sanding down her floors and restaining them. When she was done, she still had a lot to do to make the house into her dream home, but she'd done enough to take it from the House of Crazy Colors to the House of Calm, Bright, and New.

That's a more extreme example, but you can get the same fresh feeling by changing out your backsplash and painting your cabinets or painting old hand-me-down shelves and getting a slipcover for a frumpy but comfy armchair. Even just clearing out clutter and hanging a new, thrifted piece of art can refresh your space. With just a little bit of elbow grease and a whole lot of love, you can turn something that others deem trash into a most-prized treasure.

So much of decorating isn't about the price or quality of what you put into your home; it's about how everything together makes you *feel*. If you've been "meh" about your home for ages, getting up and doing a few things can revive your languid spirit. Of course, praying about it doesn't

hurt either. Talk to God about what you want your home to be and whom you want it to serve. Listen patiently for Him to reveal His plans for your home. Let God come in like a chimney sweeper to your heart and clean out all the gunk and bad thoughts you have about your home. He will do it.

So much of decorating isn't about the price or quality of what you put into your home; it's about how everything together makes you *feel.*

REFLECT

- What "named houses," famous or otherwise, inspire you? How are they good at evoking a certain feeling?
- Let's talk about the first name you thought of—the one your house might have now that you want to change. How can you pray for God to change that "message of doom" into a "message of joy"?
- How is it freeing for you to know that it's not what your house looks like that's important, but how it makes you feel? What kind of pressures can you say no to for that reason?

will do the same for you, friend. In your heart, in your home, and in your life. When it's all said and done, He gives us a new name for our homes. Mine was Restoration House, but maybe yours is House of Order or House of Bold Choices—or just good ol' *Home*. Whatever name you decide to give it or God inspires you to take, you can rest assured this place you arrive will be a place of freedom.

A LITTLE DEEPER | HOME + SOUL

Lord, thank You for creating in me the amazing ability to glorify You with the gifts You have placed in me. It's an amazing reciprocation. As I trust You, I experience life as never before. I can be free to express who You have created me to be without anxiety or fear of judgment. I can be free to create and to live a big life. All that I do is for You, on Your behalf, for Your glory. Please guide me toward a new name for my home, and give me "bouquets of roses instead of ashes, messages of joy instead of news of doom, a praising heart instead of a languid spirit" (Isaiah 61:3 MSG). Rename my home and let it be established as You display Your glory. As I walk through my house, show me in fresh ways the small things I can do to make my home a place that lives up to its name. Amen.

A NEW WAY TO DINNER

MARTHA STEWART'S VEGETABLES

CHAPTER 6

FINDING YOUR PLACE

We are God's handiwork, created in Christ Jesus to do
good works, which God prepared in advance for us to do.

—EPHESIANS 2:10

Most of the women in my life are intimidated by the word *create*. I think people are convinced that what they create won't measure up to what they picture in their mind that they become too scared to even try. The truth is, we're all creative. Whether it's snappy organizational skills or the ability to give others a chuckle and create some joy, we've all got a little something to give to others in our lives.

I've talked to so many women who want to copy something out of a magazine or blog because they don't have much confidence in their own abilities to create something from scratch. So they replicate that room they loved in the pictures they saw, but it feels sterile and flat in their own home. The flip side is all the women who tell me they have been so paralyzed by trying to make a decision that they never do; they just live with the ratty old wallpaper and mismatched furniture, hating their houses all the while.

Where you are now—the home you are in—may be no clear reflection of where you feel you are meant to be. (Remember our roach-infested studio apartment?) Now that you've explored your internal world, let's take a look at the external side of things. Practically, how do you take where you are now, settle in with it, and make a place that works for you? How do you make a place that restores you even when everything around you seems to distract?

THE JUMP-STARTING PROCESS

There is no one-size-fits-all formula, but I do have a process that helps me conquer my fears and embrace my creativity to create a home that reflects who I am and the things that are most precious to me.

1. Set a budget. This one is important for me because I pick up a lot of steam once I get started shopping. When I'm on a roll, a few extra items don't feel like much, but after decorating a whole house, those extras can add up to a lot! Setting a budget will keep you from having to expend extra energy worrying about whether you'll be able to finish what you've started with the resources you have.

2. Empty your space and donate. It's difficult to create something new and fresh when the old and dated is filling your visual space. Clear all the knickknacks, art, rugs, and furniture out of the room you are tackling. This is my family's favorite part of my design process because who

The truth is, we're all creative.

doesn't love finding throw pillows stacked on the kitchen counter or pictures leaned next to the shower? While you are clearing things out, get rid of anything you hate. I don't care if it was expensive or it's in great shape or it belonged to your great-great-great-grandmother. If looking at it makes you sad and grumpy and annoyed, it needs to go! Feeling good about what is in your space is key, so if it doesn't send you into a calm and peaceful state, say goodbye to it.

I always like to donate or pass along unwanted or unnecessary items to friends or family members, or even sell them at a garage sale. Just get them out of your space! The idea is that you're not letting something sit around just because you feel bad about throwing it out. If it's not working in your space, or even more, no longer functional, the dumpster must become your bestie. However, if you hate the thing but another beloved member of your household loves the thing, remember that no furniture or item is worth the peace of your marriage or relationship. So sometimes we just have to find a way to compromise. If you can't offload it, have some frank discussions about repurposing, slipcovering, painting, or breathing new life into an old item. Be nice, but discuss the practicalities of an item and what it does to you. Together you'll find a way to bring both peace and functionality into your shared situation.

3. Think on it. Sit down in that nice empty space and hang out there for a bit. Think of the most important function or functions the room will need to serve. If you have a huge family and host gatherings frequently, your dining room likely needs to hold a crowd. It also might need to be flexible in terms of decor to fit the season. I'm one for simple and clean, but if farmhouse or more traditional is your style, do what's right for you. Even if your personal style leans toward rustic, there are ways to keep

things minimal while still nodding to your love for all things warm and cozy. Your living room might need to be the perfect spot to hold your teenage sons and their friends for after-school video game tournaments and serve as a casual spot for your weekly moms' group. Or maybe your spare bedroom needs to act as an office *and* a guest space.

To keep it simple, edit any pieces or decorative items that you just can't seem to make fit. Don't be afraid to store things away for a season and bring them back. I can't tell you how many times I've wanted to discard pieces just because they visually frustrate me but have decided to stash them in a safe place and come back around to them later. Magically, some of those same items that didn't quite make the cut in one season, I can't live without in the next.

Once you have the room's functions defined, you can start looking for furniture that will serve those functions: a big, expandable dining table with chairs that are easy to store when not in use or a couch with a durable, washable slipcover that can stand up to spilled snacks and teen boy sweat, or even a small desk with lots of storage to keep office papers out of sight when your in-laws come to visit. Focus on the most important and largest pieces you'll need. Maybe you already have something perfect (or that will be perfect once it's spruced up). Maybe you need to shop. Either way, once you have those pieces (they don't have to be finished!), bring them back into the space. Take your time, move them around, and figure out the best spots for them. Large pieces like sofas, chairs, consoles, and tables will serve as your room's anchors. No matter what else you bring in, the rule is that it has to work with these!

4. Shop your space. With your anchors in place, go shopping through your own stuff. Piece by piece, go through all that stuff you moved out of the room at the beginning, and decide what will come back into the room by asking yourself a few questions.

- Does this piece serve the room's function?
- Does it work with the anchor pieces?
- Does this item make me happy—is it beautiful? Or sentimental? Or does it make me laugh?

Hopefully the items you bring back in will elicit a resounding "yes!" to all three questions, but you may have some functional items that don't make you especially happy, or something that makes you super happy but doesn't serve much of a purpose—and that's okay too! Bring your "yes" items back in and find homes for them.

5. Bring on the color. At this point, you have enough decided to pick some colors. If you already love the paint and furniture colors you have, awesome; skip this step. If not, look at your anchors and use them to help you determine a color palette. Pick a color you love to start, even if it's not what you are seeing in every magazine. Colors go in and out of style, but you live in this house, so you should love your walls, trends or no trends! If you are hesitant to go for a big, bold color, you really can't go wrong with white (my personal favorite) or gray walls. A nice greige (that's gray and beige mixed) has a warmer tone than traditional gray and is pretty universally liked. A neutral wall color will allow you to have fun with various colors in accessories and art.

With paint done and your main pieces in place, you can get a good sense of what you are missing. A word of advice: you do not—I repeat: you do *not*—need to hop in your car, go straight to Target or Pottery

MULTIFUNCTIONAL SPACES

Just about every home could use a little more space—an extra bedroom set aside exclusively for guests or a nice roomy office space or home gym. But, let's be honest, most of us don't have four thousand square feet to play with, which means a lot of our rooms need to serve more than one purpose. Creating a multifunctional space isn't always easy. When considering how to divide a space, especially if it's small, you will want to select every piece of furniture and decor very carefully. Everything should serve more than one purpose.

+ A sofa bed or stylish futon can be used for both seating and sleeping in spaces where you'll need to host overnight guests from time to time.

+ Side tables with storage built in are great for holding items that only need occasional use, such as books that aren't that pretty or tabletop-worthy or those coasters that have nostalgic significance but aren't that easy on the eyes.

+ A fold-down desk makes it easy to tuck away office space in a room that needs to pull double duty.

+ A fold-down treadmill can slide beneath a bed when not in use.

+ Under-bed storage containers are easily hidden but can be pulled out quickly, making them ideal to store things like extra linens, beach towels, or wrapping paper and other seasonal items.

Barn or Crate & Barrel, and fill your cart with every single thing you think you are missing for your home. It's okay to live with an empty room for a little while. Take your time finding items to fill those holes. You want the room to be a reflection of you and your family. The final layer of things you add to the room should be personal and speak to your identity. This will—and should—take time.

YOUR IDENTITY IN YOUR HOME

That final layer of identity is something only you—and no one else—can make in an authentic way. It doesn't have to be a complicated process; you can relax into it and let it happen naturally over time.

1. All the Things

When creating an environment in your home that speaks to your soul, it's important to make it personal. Old family photos or treasures always add warmth and a feeling of connection, but if you don't have anything significant that's been passed down to you, that's no problem. Don't be afraid to get out, shake off the dust, and shop your local vintage and antique shops or even estate and garage sales. They even have estate sales online now! I have found so many amazing gems in thrift shops that adorn the walls of our home today. These little things add that extra bit of character and personality to your space and are awesome conversation starters.

2. Plant Life

Beyond planting seeds of community in those who enter your home, you're going to want some real, live plant life. Adding plants to your home is a great way to add character and texture and bring life to your

space. Be sure to choose plants that fit your home aesthetic and your care personality. If you have a black thumb, stick to hardy houseplants that are almost impossible to kill. Take it from me: if you are a plant novice, don't start with a Fiddle-Leaf Fig or any other plant that requires extra care and attention to survive. Your local nursery can help you find the perfect options for your space, budget, and commitment level!

3. Memories and Promises

Shared positive memories are some of the best glue for holding a family together. Art doesn't have to mean a professional painting that costs big bucks. It can be your favorite picture from a vacation, printed large and framed. Or the art project your kid did that makes you smile displayed in a shadow box. You can even hit up a painting or pottery class as a family to create something together. One of my favorite things to do is to print poster-size images of my kiddos, whether professional quality or shot with my phone, and have them printed via our local office supply or drug store. It's super cheap, and because of the larger size, it feels like art in the home. But it's more personal than art, of course, because the faces belong to people who actually *live* in the house.

You could also take it a step further and work on nurturing those memories in other ways. For instance, buy a pretty journal and place it on your nightstand. As often as you can remember, recall the good things in life and write them down. It doesn't have to be a dissertation or a blog entry. Some days you'll just be able to write a sentence, and some days you will want to add more. This isn't meant to be a journal, just a quick way to remind yourself of all the good things God has done in your life and all that He has promised to do. It could turn into a priceless family heirloom to hand down.

LOW-MAINTENANCE PLANT OPTIONS

LOW-LIGHT PLANTS

Take it from this Seattle girl: I know all too well the woes of living in a home with low light. Seven to eight months out of the year, we struggle to find sun around here. Here are a few plants that are perfectly low maintenance and don't require a ton of natural light:

+ ZZ PLANT | Boasting a uniquely shaped, waxy leaf, the ZZ plant is a favorite and is hearty to the core. It doesn't ask for much—just a little water and light every now and then.

+ INDOOR PALM VARIETIES | There are so many options, but try going for a smaller variety like Parlor or Ponytail varieties.

+ BOSTON FERN | A great traditional option that needs humidity and mist but functions well indoors and doesn't need a ton of attention. Just be sure to keep the dead fronds pruned and this one should be happy for years.

+ MONSTERA | This plant gives the space a light tropical feel but will not overwhelm it like the palm.

+ PRAYER PLANT | This beauty is variegated, offers color and texture, and is low maintenance.

LOW-WATER PLANTS

These days it's so easy with our schedules to forget to take care of those little indoor plants that take care of us. While there are so many contraptions and devices on the market to help remind us when to water our little buddies, I tend to lean toward indoor plants that just flat-out don't require much H_2O to begin with. Here are a few of my faves:

+ SNAKE PLANT | This one's not what you think, although the tips of the leaves look a bit like the head of a cobra, which is probably where the name comes from. What I love about this one is the color variation of the leaves and how they can add personality and character to a shelf, a side table, or the floor of any room in your home.

+ SAGO PALM | The Sago is one of my favorite palms, mostly because I consider it the "wonder of palms." The branches grow compact and neat and complement just about any interior perfectly.

+ SPIDER PLANT | This plant can be contained in a pot on the floor, but if you want to kick it up a notch, hang it to allow the tendrils to grow up or down toward the floor.

+ SUCCULENTS | This whole variety has gained popularity over the past few years, and I am not one bit mad about it. Not only do they require little to no water at all, depending on the type, they are just the cutest little things and come in some pretty eclectic colors, shapes, and sizes.

REFLECT

- Have you ever tried to replicate a design idea and it didn't work for you? Why was that? What might have worked instead, in light of your personal home story?
- Do you have trouble living with an unfinished space? Why or why not? What good might come of living with an unfinished space until you find the right things to put in it?
- Before you roll up your sleeves to tackle a room, identify five things you want to say goodbye to and five things you want to keep. How have these things fit in to the story you want to tell? Or how do they no longer fit?

A LITTLE DEEPER | HOME + SOUL

God, help us know who we are. Help us to find our identities in You, then watch that unfold in our homes. Help us know that our homes are more than buildings that house people and welcome people in. Our homes, much like our own selves, are meant to remind us of Your faithfulness, Your goodness, and Your purpose in our lives. Restore to us the joy of home, God. Help us to see our homes as Yours before our own. Thank You. Amen.

A FEW OF THE GOOD THINGS IN MY LIFE:

_____

_____

_____

_____

_____

_____

_____

_____

_____

_____

_____

CHAPTER 7

LET YOUR SENSES GUIDE YOU

Ears that hear and eyes that see—
the Lord *has made them both.*

—PROVERBS 20:12

Have you ever walked into someone's home and just felt relaxed? At peace? On the surface of it all, it might seem that the thirty-inch-deep sofa and down-filled pillows would be the reason, but upon further inspection, and after more time and conversation, you find that it's the heart of the people inside that does it. Their lives are reflected in their home. The way they make you feel comfortable and cared for beckons you to stay just a little while longer. To linger. To fill your time with the important things in life like people, stories, memories, and healing.

Creating a restored home, the kind that makes you want to return over and over again, is as much about making everyone who enters feel cared for and comfortable as it is about creating a beautiful space. I'm not saying the aesthetics don't matter—we're visual creatures, after all. A lovely space can certainly entice you to linger. But carefully curated rooms are only part of the equation. It's important to include all our senses! Soft pillows and throws can encourage after-dinner lounging and conversation, the sweet smell of freshly baked cookies can take us back to childhood and make us more open and receptive to friendship, and the sounds of soft music can provide the perfect soundtrack to deep conversations.

Creating a restored home is as much about making everyone who enters feel cared for and comfortable as it is about creating a beautiful space.

As you make decisions about what to put in your home, think about it from a whole-body perspective for everyone who lives and visits there. That leather sofa might be gorgeous but not terribly comfortable for the Sunday afternoon naps your husband loves, and that rustic farmhouse bench might make you feel like your favorite HGTV star, but the lack of back support means that your guests will wrap up dinner quickly to

avoid back pain. Alternatively, it's probably worth buying that super-soft velvet wingback chair that might not be quite the style you wanted but is so comfortable you know it will be everyone's favorite spot.

Whether it's your guests, yourself, or the ones who share your home, everyone feels a little more cherished and cared for when we take the time to think about each of our five senses. Here are a few ways that you can engage them all.

SMELL

It's harder in the winter months, but when spring and summer beckon the great outdoors in, open the windows. I love opening our windows in the spring to show the funk of winter the exit and let all things spring inside. The fresh air is inviting and invigorating, and the smells from the outdoors are wonderful for pepping up any mood in a home. When the weather doesn't allow open windows, use candles or essential oil diffusers to lightly scent your home. If using different scents in different areas, try to choose complementary smells so your house doesn't start to smell like a Yankee Candle shop! When using essential oils, choose those of higher grade that will aid in stimulating the whole system instead of just smelling good. Candles are no different—choose soy candles that contain only natural ingredients for full effectiveness.

TOUCH AND SIGHT

Any home stylist or designer will tell you that visual texture is a big deal in the home. Adding texture not only offers visual variety and helps the eye move around a room, but it also creates warmth in many ways. There are many different ways to accomplish this, but one of the easiest and my favorite is the addition of rugs and throw pillows. I like to change things out in my home pretty often. Changing small things like accent rugs and throw pillows is an easy way to add variety without breaking the bank.

When choosing rugs and pillows, try to go for mostly neutral. This way, you can easily mix and match, add patterns, and not have to spend more than necessary on changing the entire space based on something temporary.

Aside from visual texture, we can fill our homes with tactile texture. A soft fur pillow, smooth reclaimed wood, rough coral—things that invite us to touch and interact with them help us to feel grounded in the space.

SOUND

We're going back to the windows here. Bring in the sounds of the outdoors as well. Nothing beats the blues more than the sounds of birds chirping or kids playing outdoors. They help lighten the mood of your heart and home.

If you're not a fan of open windows because of allergies or inclement weather, try turning on your radio or hooking up a Bluetooth speaker and searching for a sounds-of-summer station on your favorite subscription service, or just crank up the music!

In our home music is kind of a big deal. I find that our kids just can't keep themselves still (in the best way) whenever we turn on the tunes. I constantly have music on as I work around the house. Like Snow White sang, "Whistle While You Work"!

A WORLD OF SCENTS

It's amazing how the right scent can bring a space to life. After all, what's the biggest thing in the room? The air! You can strategically choose a palette of scents to help create the mood you want, whether it's with candles, oils, or other diffusers. Just remember: a little goes a long way. Easy does it. And start with a base of fresh, clean air in a fresh, clean home.

When choosing essential oils, while the cheaper ones from your local grocer may be tempting, you'll want to look for oils that are 100 percent pure with no additives and as close as possible to the source they were pulled from. Also, instead of shopping local discount stores or your grocer for them, try your hand at online businesses that specialize in the production and harvesting of the oils or your local natural pharmaceutical establishment or health food shop. Just a few drops of these scents in a candle or diffuser, and you'll be feeling the effects in your space.

CALM

Lavender	Pine	Lemongrass
Sandalwood	Rosemary	

ALERT

Cinnamon	Basil	Ginger
Grapefruit or citrus	Peppermint	

HAPPY

Vanilla	Geranium	Sandalwood
Jasmine	Rose	Any sort of cookie baking

Find a music service that best fits your budget and subscribe. I recommend subscribing because you have a lot more control over what you and your kiddos listen to. Select a station, get your groove on, and shake off the blues.

Don't be afraid to break out of your norm. If you're a diehard country music fan, give some R & B music or jazz a try.

You'll be surprised what your body will do and what your ears will be satisfied by when you try something new.

TASTE

Food sets the mood. It also offers us the unique opportunity to continue beautifying our tables and spaces with an array of colors and shapes. Part of building a restorative space means gathering others to you. Nothing does that like food. And nothing gives you energy or empowers you to connect more than food either. Wouldn't you agree? I mean, all you have to do is bring out a platter of cheese or a fun snack tray and the smiles on faces are endless. I personally love a good charcuterie board. I haven't met *one* person yet who doesn't love eating one or one host who doesn't love making one and putting her own spin on it. Whether you use an official board or a salvaged, clean plank of wood purchased from your local hardware store, there are so many ways to give this crowd-pleasing side-turned-main-dish some life.

The fun thing about these boards is that there are no hard, fast rules. That's always a draw for me for just about anything when it comes to hosting. Your traditional charcuterie board will consist of a meat assortment, a selection of cheeses and crackers, and a few spreads for guests to choose from. Whether you're a salami lover or not, there are many cured

MY MUST-HAVE SEASONAL ITEMS

WINTER

+ A good, smoky scented candle like wood fire, cedarwood, vetiver, or any combo of the three
+ A cozy wool coat or jacket
+ A firepit
+ A cozy pair of pants and slippers for lounging around the house on days spent inside
+ An electric blanket

SPRING

+ Fresh market or grocery store flowers
+ New throw pillows
+ Lighter bedding/duvet/comforter
+ New window treatments (think less heavy; sheer panels or light cotton are great options)
+ New doormat

SUMMER

+ Hammock
+ Lightweight throws
+ Colorful throw pillows
+ Vases and planters for freshly picked flowers
+ Fresh, crisply scented candles with hints of citrus or herbs like basil

FALL

+ Cozy wool throws
+ Candles highlighted with scents of cinnamon or clove
+ Fresh, new area rugs in an entry or communal living spaces
+ An insulated container for hot cider or tea
+ A quality Dutch oven for all those roasts and stews

meat options—fresh and packaged—to serve your guests. As for cheese, we all know the choices are endless. You'll want to have at least one of each type: firm (like a cheddar), soft (like a Brie or goat), and aged (like a Gorgonzola or Stilton). Spreads these days are offered in a variety of flavor combinations. Fig spread is one of my favorites, but don't be afraid to either make your own or step out of what you normally gravitate toward and mix up the flavors.

After you've laid out all of your main items (you can just haphazardly toss them on the board in a pattern of your choice), you will want to add pickled foods like cornichons (petite pickles), carrots, beans, or even red onions along with dried nuts and fruits like almonds and apricots or figs.

Trust your instinct when setting everything out on the board and just go with your gut. You are guaranteed to overthink it if you're a type A like me. Don't. Let your creative soul run wild, and enjoy serving your friends and family fun and easy appetizers or a meal they'll surely ask for again.

Friends, we were created to indulge in good food while forging friendships. Don't neglect this one when you or others in your home may need a pick-me-up.

Good food really doesn't need to be fancy. I can't tell you how many times I've cut up some fresh fruit, opened a container of hummus, and thrown some crackers and salami into bowls. Just a little bit of effort, and my family and friends felt loved and cared for.

———

No matter who you are, how much skill you have, or whether or not you're an ace at making the home environment you want, you have the

automatic gift of your five senses. God gave them to you for you to enjoy the world He made. If you ever feel stuck while making your holistic home, you can always go back to your senses and jumpstart your direction. What sounds would uplift you? What smells would calm you? What textures and colors would soothe you or perk you up? What tastes would nourish you or make your loved ones feel welcome? Use your internal compass, and you'll find yourself building an environment that speaks to the whole person, welcoming every one of the senses and the people God has given you.

REFLECT

- Look around your house now. Can you find an item that brings joy to you through each of your five senses? What is it about each item that speaks to you?
- What sounds do you find medicinal? Pinpoint a musical artist or album that makes you feel (1) calm, (2) energized, (3) unwound, (4) cheered, (5) positive, and (6) thoughtful, and make sure they're cued up and ready to deploy in your space.
- How could using all your senses, rather than just your eyes, on the next thing you bring into your home change what you choose or gravitate toward? What new possibilities might it open up to you?

A LITTLE DEEPER | HOME + SOUL

Father, thank You for giving me my senses, my preferences, and my tastes, and for gifting the ones in my home with these same miraculous powers. We so want to enjoy Your world together. Show me how to listen and cater to the senses You gave me, using them to choose carefully the items that make up our environment. I want to make a space that brings comfort and peace through every sense. It's one of the ways I want to worship You. Amen.

MIX-AND-MATCH CHARCUTERIE BOARD SHOPPING LIST

HARDWARE

Board or boards (marble or
  wood is best)

Small bowls or receptacles
  for wet items

Cheese knives and forks

Party picks

Side plates (determine the size
  based on how quickly you want
  the food to be gone!)

Plenty of napkins

SOFTWARE

Really, anything goes here. Mix and match from these categories to get yourself started, but the more you do it, the more you'll discover what your taste buds like most. I'd choose three from each category, but the sky is truly the limit.

MEAT

Salami

Mortadella

Smoked ham

Prosciutto

Roast beef

Herbed turkey

Pâté

Sausage bites

CHEESE (FIRM OR HARD)

Cheddar

Gouda

Muenster

Manchego

Good quality Parmesan

CHEESE (SOFT)

Brie

Camembert

Goat

Boursin or herbed cheese

Sheep milk cheese

CHEESE (AGED)

Gorgonzola

Stilton

Roquefort

Taleggio

CRACKERS + BREAD

Cheese straws (great for
  draping with prosciutto)

Platter-shaped water crackers

Basket of baguette slices (if you're
  going for a meal option)

Rougher breadlike wafers

Classic butter crackers

SPREADS

Fig

Hot pepper jelly (especially with
  cream cheese)

Apple butter

Pear preserves

Raspberry

Chutney

Mustard

PICKLED GARNISHES

Olives

Pickled onions

Cornichons

Pickled beans or carrots

Pickled radishes

Caper berries

DRY GARNISHES

Almonds

Cashews

Shelled pistachios

Walnuts

Dried apples

Candied nuts

Raisins

Dried cranberries

Figs

CHAPTER 8

MAKING SPACE FOR GOD

Come near to God and he will come near to you.

—JAMES 4:8

Humans are doers and makers by nature. We want to accomplish things. We set lofty goals to better ourselves and fulfill lifetime dreams. We have ambitions, and it takes a lot to stop us from running full force to achieve them.

This way of thinking, I've found, is really no different when it comes to our homes. You probably have ambitions for your space as well. You've started to explore your story, and in this section you've learned some practical steps for making your home a sanctuary for yourself and your loved ones. Now, before we move on, let's re-center back on the basis of this reality: our home at its core is a space for communion with God.

Sure, when it comes to our home ambitions, it's easy to spend ridiculous amounts of time scouring Pinterest, Instagram, blogs, and magazines—pinning paint colors and fabric swatches, drooling over our dream couch or watching for that perfect lamp to go on sale so it's in our budget. We spend time and energy shopping, arranging, rearranging, painting, and then do it all over again a few years later. And of course, we want to share our accomplishments, basking in the short-lived glow of likes and thumbs-ups as they come rolling in on social media. But it never lasts long. Before we know it, we're back to lusting after new throw pillows or looking for another space to refinish to show off, when the truth of the matter is that all we truly crave and seek is authentic, genuine community and relationship in our *real* lives. Relate?

Well, I've spent an unmentionable amount of time over my thirty-plus years of life dreaming of home and thinking of all the ways it would or should be. I've thought of how it would look, feel, smell, and even sound, but as you'll recall, not much of that time was spent asking God His opinion about any of that until recently. If we're not careful, we begin to place value in getting things "just right" instead of making sure our hearts are *in* the right place.

If we're not careful, we begin to place value in getting things "just right" instead of making sure our hearts are *in* the right place.

Am I saying that you have to doggedly kneel in prayer, asking God what your next move should be for pillows or that new rug? No. Most of my prayer about our home is centered on my expression of the type of home I want our family to have, a desire He has honestly already placed in my heart. Those prayers renew those desires in me and provide valuable check-ins for whether or not I'm on track.

CHOOSING PEACE OVER CHAOS

When we first moved into our current home, I was less than impressed with the overall architecture and aesthetics of the space. It took me a little while to gather my emotions and settle in to the fact that the only way I'd truly be at peace would be to turn lemons into lemonade and start making this place a home. Our home. I knew what God had already placed in my heart for this home. I knew we wanted it to be a place where people felt welcome and accepted. It would be a place that wasn't only aesthetically pleasing to those who entered but would speak to their weary souls in more ways than one. Those were the things that were important to me, and, on many occasions, God and I talked about it. It was a sincere and earnest prayer of my heart that became a reality as I trusted Him and not the *things* I chose to bring into the house.

I've also learned the hard way that when I choose to do the opposite, it yields nothing but confusion and chaos. What is the point of that unrest, and what price am I willing to pay for peace? To avoid being distracted in this way, I have often had to remind myself of what is amazing about our home; and the answer is never what we sit on or walk on, but the people who fill it.

Sometimes that peace for me has come in the form of choosing to step away from distractions around me like extra social events (as much as I love a good party), overcommitting to hosting events, or volunteering for too many projects with church or the kids' schools. Sometimes that peace looks like disconnecting from reading things that don't help invigorate or revive my creative process.

Try taking a moment to evaluate your level of peace, and edit some things in your life that may be sucking the life right out of you. Chances are, without my mentioning a word, you already know what those things are.

Think about Mary and Martha. Give me a woman alive who hasn't cringed at that story a little. I bet you know it, and the moral of the story: that our time with God is the most important thing. This is what Mary chose.

Jesus even said to Martha: "Martha, Martha . . . you are worried and upset about many things, but few things are needed—or indeed only one. Mary has chosen what is better, and it will not be taken away from her" (Luke 10:41–42). Mary chose to sit at the feet of Jesus and make Him her restful and peaceful place for that time.

But again, cringe. Of course, time with God is most important. We know this, but we also know everyone has to eat, so food has to be prepared, dishes and pots and pans need to be washed, and kids have to be cared for. Choosing God over all of the things we have to do isn't the easiest feat. It's not easy to break away from all the e-mails, the overtime, the friends, the piles of laundry, the never-ending meal planning, or the shuttling of kids. Life calls, and most times, depending on the season of life, it screams obnoxiously until we answer.

Mary, however, didn't consider the time that Jesus was there to be an interruption. Instead, it was a time to reflect, relate, and be still, knowing

I have often had to remind myself of what is amazing about our home; and the answer is never what we sit on or walk on, but the people who fill it.

that she could trust God to ensure that the other things that needed to be taken care of would ultimately be handled.

There's a lot of discussion around this popular Bible story, especially among many women who tend to lean more toward a Martha mentality. (Don't worry, girls, I am right there with you.)

I tend to concern myself too much with what's not done in my home or what needs to be done. And I find that the more and more I choose to do that, the softer the voice of God becomes in my life. It then becomes easier and easier to *do* instead of just *be*.

In our homes, we are meant to live—no doubt. But there is so much more to how we live in our homes with the people we love than what we do alone.

A PLACE FOR DETOX

I'd like to think Mary was doing the most needed type of detox and perhaps the best kind of all—detox for her soul. She found it by sitting at the feet of Jesus.

Sometimes this is just what we need. Well, maybe more than sometimes. We need it *all* the time, but life is fast-paced. Our schedules are weighted by tasks and our brains overloaded by the incomplete and the yet to begin. I don't think God is as concerned with those things as we tend to become. He wants us, beckons even, to come and sit at His feet for a while. Somehow when we choose that needed thing, everything else seems to melt away and those lists are the least of our concerns. It frees up our souls to soar and be more productive in our days and more purposeful in the way we live. It's what we were created for, and there's no peace in this world like it that any temporary fix can give.

MY READING LIST | STAPLES

+ *Chasing Slow* by Erin Loechner
+ *I'm Still Here* by Austin Channing Brown
+ The *She Reads Truth Bible*, from the general editors of *She Reads Truth* and Holman Bibles
+ *Homebody* by Joanna Gaines
+ *In the Company of Women* by Grace Bonney
+ *Wild and Free* by Jess Connolly and Hayley Morgan
+ *The New Bohemians* by Justina Blakeney
+ *Domino: Your Guide to a Stylish Home*, from the editors of *domino* magazine
+ *We Were Eight Years in Power* by Ta-Nehisi Coates
+ *Living with Pattern* by Rebecca Atwood

I want to encourage you to create a space in your home for sitting at Jesus' feet. This should be a space you can't wait to get away to—somewhere reserved for communing with God and maybe reading your favorite books or whatever you choose to do at that time. I always think I can have quiet time anywhere (and I can if I try hard enough), but when I'm sitting at the kitchen table my mind wanders to the dishes in the sink or the grocery shopping I need to do later. Ditto with the living room and the basket of kids' toys that need to be put away and the basket of laundry I need to fold. It's easier to take the time we need with God when we are intentional about setting the stage to do so.

This spot should be cozy and beautiful—even if it's just a comfy chair with a side table to hold your Bible and a pretty houseplant. Place the chair toward a lovely view out the window or facing a piece of art you've always loved. Make it the spot in the house you long to be, and you'll find yourself there often. Remember that you're not striving for perfection here; this is a place where you come to shed that and all the other weights you carry. But it should be a space that fits *you* and fits you well.

> This spot should be cozy and beautiful—even if it's just a comfy chair with a side table to hold your Bible and a pretty houseplant.

A PLACE TO DREAM

This spot can also be the perfect place in your home where you can dream and get cozy with your favorite pillows, throws, books, and journals. This will be the space where you write, pray, laugh, and sit silently, so you want it to be comfy and cute! If you don't have the extra space in your home, this may be a breakfast nook or a special chair in the corner of a bedroom. Wherever you choose to bring this place to life, make it your own. Add your favorite scented candles and keep your special pens and pencils tucked away in a personalized container. With my love for antique

STYLE A BEDSIDE TABLE | 3 EASY STEPS

1. Clear the table of all items including lighting.
2. Edit pieces by deciding what will be used most often. For instance, when styling your bedside table, you may want to set out a small dish for jewelry or use a tray of some sort to keep everything in one place.
3. Layer items that add personality. Choose unique or personal items, such as two or three of your favorite books or a small container or vase for fresh florals. Then choose a lamp, which will add flavor and personality.

When we feel life is overwhelming, we need Him to hold our hands tighter.

and vintage items, I'd probably add found items from local antique shops to fill this role. If you prefer new, shop your favorite stores and buy a few accessories that really speak to you and make you feel good.

A PLACE TO REACH OUT YOUR HAND

I am certain God uses our kids to grow us into our whole, healed, and put-together selves. He used one of mine to remind me why we need to make time and space to be with God in the first place.

A few years back I was out shopping with one of our four kiddos. We've always taught our kids to hold our hands in the parking lot, so it's second nature for them. They just take hold when we begin to step out. We now have older children who don't need to hand-hold in parking lots, but the illustration is still applicable and practical. We normally never needed to ask them; it was a knee-jerk reaction whenever we prepared to walk to or from our car.

On that day, as we began to walk toward our car, my son grabbed my hand. As we got closer to the car, he squeezed my hand tightly, looked up at me, and said, "Mommy, could you hold my hand a little tighter please?"

I asked him why. His explanation blew me away.

"Sometimes I want to let go and run into the parking lot, so I need you to hold my hand tighter so I don't let go."

Wow. Friends, there are some lessons here for us.

Naturally, I know that our kids need and seek healthy boundaries in their lives. They need to know that they are safe, loved, and secure in order to grow into the amazing human beings God has created them to be. I get that. I can't help but compare what happened in that parking lot on that day to my relationship with God, our Creator.

Like my son, sometimes I just need God to hold my hand a little tighter. I just need to feel Him and be reminded that He is there and looking out for me.

When we feel life is overwhelming, we need Him to hold our hands tighter.

When we cannot make a decision or feel tossed to and fro, we need God to hold our hands a little tighter.

When we are fearful and don't want to do something, we know He has purposed us to do, we need Him to hold our hands a little tighter.

When all the things in life seem chaotic, crazy, and just a little frazzled? You've got it, we need Him to hold our hands, our lives, our hearts just a little tighter.

We all know that doubt and confusion can creep in at any given moment and steal away our ability to reason. We get so captivated by the wrong things and take so many things and people for granted. Life

A LITTLE DEEPER | HOME + SOUL

God, I love that You want to be near me. Not only do I want to be close to You, but I need Your presence on my most basic level. When I make my space to approach You, please meet me there. Pull me away from all my Martha activities, and help me choose Your peace over my never-ending flow of concerns and distractions. Please bless and consecrate that time and space, and reach out to hold my hand tighter every time I enter it. Amen.

RECLAIMED SPACES

Look for opportunities to find some dead space in your home that you can make yours again. Is it that little nook that needs that throw you've been eyeing online for months? Or perhaps it's that blank wall begging for some of your favorite art (e.g., your kids' artwork) and those family photos that have been hidden for far too long. In reclaiming these spaces, you incorporate more of you into your home and create a cozier and more personal living environment.

RECLAIMED MOMENTS

Can't seem to break away? Pop on some of your favorite devotional music while washing dishes or executing household chores. I know dedicated quiet time or worship time may be a hard thought for some of us type A folks out there (raises hand), but in the long run, it's so worth it to fill your soul with things that matter even if it's in the middle of daytime tasks. Not only will this lend a helping hand to your spirit, but it will also help you get through your to-dos just a tad more quickly.

becomes stale and lonely and hard—and this, in no way, is the full life that we have been called to live and pour into others.

As a visual reminder, you can place a symbolic object in your quiet place that reminds you to reach for Him—or to pray for anything for that matter. You might choose a growing plant for your kids, a beautiful river stone for a family member, or a special candle holder to remind you to pray for that issue you keep bringing to Him over and over. Let your space prompt you to keep returning, again and again, to the One who keeps a firm hold of your hand and heart.

When we make time to be with God, we remember that daily (or maybe even by the minute), we can reach out to Him and ask Him to hold our hands a little bit tighter.

REFLECT

- What would you say is your best environment for finding closeness with God? Have you felt close to Him in the past in any special place, like a retreat or in nature? How can you reflect or re-create this in your quiet space?
- What things tend to distract you from time with God? How can you fortify and protect your space (and time) against these things?
- In what situations do you often feel like you're going to "run off into the parking lot," when you need God to hold you tighter? How does regular quiet time with Him help you prepare for these situations?

PART 3

SHARING YOUR RESTORED HOME

"I alone cannot change the world, but I can cast a stone across the waters to create many ripples."

—MOTHER TERESA

CHAPTER 9

THE POWER OF THE IMPERFECT

He said to me, "My grace is sufficient for you, for my power is made perfect in weakness."

–2 CORINTHIANS 12:9

've pretty much been a perfectionist my entire life. This has been both a strength and a weakness. And with the birth of each child, move from each home, and addition of each year, I've learned how to manage it more.

I've learned how to let go of a lot of things that didn't ever matter much at all. Perfectly vacuumed lines in the carpet—not needed. Dirty dishes in the sink—not such a big deal anymore. We have much bigger fish to fry these days, and I have decided to make a conscious decision each and every day that I will do my absolute best to make the most of the time we have left with our kiddos in the house.

Letting go of needing to have my house perfectly styled and perfectly clean and perfectly *perfect* all the time has had an impact I never expected. You see, my home is never cleaner or more styled or more perfect than when I'm having company come over. It doesn't matter if it's my best friend or the queen of England coming for a visit—you can safely bet you'll find me cleaning and tidying and tweaking and hiding clutter for hours before that doorbell rings. It's difficult to shake that perfectionist streak when company is involved! Of course, I want my guests to think well of me and to have a wonderful experience in my home. I want them to focus on the sparkling conversation, not smudges on my windows. I want them to feel comfortable on my sofa, not distracted by the pile of mail on the console table. But I've realized there's a balance.

Trying to appear perfect for my guests is exhausting, and all that cleaning and prepping and stressing leaves me too distracted to focus on the matter at hand. Instead of preparing myself to connect with my guests and open up to them, I'm grinning through gritted teeth when I notice a spot I missed with the vacuum!

Guests seem more relaxed and comfortable now that my home feels more like we actually, you know, live here!

So I've consciously let that perfectionism go when hosting. I still tidy up, but my house no longer looks like a magazine layout when guests arrive. There might be mail on the console table or a basket of toys by the sofa. But you know what? It hasn't hurt my gatherings one bit. If anything, I've noticed that guests seem more relaxed and comfortable now that my home feels more like we actually, you know, live here!

WELCOMING THE *GREAT PERFECTER*

I know I don't always get it right. At times I still find myself obsessing over keeping everything just so, even when I know it doesn't really matter. It's almost as if I think that making everything around me perfect will make me more perfect too, even though I know—I *know*—perfection is only found in God.

Sometimes I am needy.

I yell at my kids from time to time.

I am late.

I am impatient and sometimes just downright mean.

"But he said to me, 'My grace is sufficient for you, for my power is made perfect in weakness.' Therefore I will boast all the more gladly about my weaknesses, so that Christ's power may rest on me. That is why, for Christ's sake, I delight in weaknesses, in insults, in hardships, in persecutions, in difficulties. For when I am weak, then I am strong" (2 Corinthians 12:9–10).

In my weakness, He has made me strong. This, friends, is the power of imperfection: that our lives would be made new. That our minds would be refreshed and our souls would be made whole. That our homes would,

IT DOESN'T HAVE TO BE PERFECT

I've learned a bit over time to just embrace the not-so-new things in our homes. Years ago it was the chippy imperfection of a sideboard or dresser. Today, it's the tousled pillows on our sofa, crumbs and pen marks on our dining table, and chips on the baseboards. Whatever your ideal of perfection is in your home, try embracing all the little things that make your home yours.

as a result, be filled with peace; and that we would learn to rest in Him, with each and every imperfection and each and every day.

There is nothing more true or pure than a heart that trusts in Him. He comes alongside us in those times when we need it most: when our faith is weak and our confidence is low. He takes all our worries, our weaknesses, our imperfections, and dims the light on them to magnify all the wonderful gifts He has placed in us. And in that, there is power to accept the imperfections not just in yourself, but in your home.

Just like yourself, your home was never meant to be perfect. The *Great Perfecter* is the only One who can come in and make your house feel like home, perfecting it all in His time.

> Just like yourself, your home was never meant to be perfect. The *Great Perfecter* is the only One who can come in and make your house feel like home, perfecting it all in His time.

While most of my plans often fall to the wayside and things typically never work out the way I intend, His plans have prevailed in my life, especially in His calling for me and for our home. So I can say from experience, when you let go of perfection in your home, you make room for blessings to follow.

So far in this journey we have looked at restoring our own stories and restoring our homes for our families and ourselves. Now we'll explore opening our homes as restorative spaces for guests and community. As usual, that process starts internally—with letting go of the things that hold us back. We'll get so much joy out of a home full of warmth and community when we say no to holding ourselves to impossible standards before we let anyone in. We won't worry if our stuff is nice enough or be embarrassed about what's not picture-perfect. When we invite others in with open hearts, we'll start to realize all that we actually already have.

WE ARE RICH

A couple of years ago I was spending time with a friend. Our kids were in and out of the house and the backyard, up and down the stairs, on and off the potty, and yet for some reason on that day, we didn't mind all the commotion one bit. Our conversation was full and deep and carried along by big mugs of coffee. Coffee is always a good thing to add to conversations around here. It just makes things better.

Just as we realized our precious time was coming to a close, I took a deep breath and said, "Ah, we are so rich."

Thinking of life in this way isn't always easy for me. I meet these people from time to time who just seem overwhelmingly happy and joyful and always see the positive side of things. Me—on the other hand—I've always felt like I've had to fight for my joy. Maybe it was connected to my need for things to be perfect. I have had to fight to see the good in things and in people. I am always quick to notice the things I don't have, the

CREATE A PLACE OF PEACE

Maybe it's your sofa or even the kitchen table. Whenever I have people over for coffee, I always like to make things cozy and create a space that feels warm and welcoming. If it's winter, the fire is always going. If it's summer, the blinds, and sometimes the windows, are open to allow the fresh breeze in. Creating mini-retreat spaces in your living room is a great way to encourage your family and friends to just relax and let it all go. Whatever the case may be and whatever the season, fill your chairs and sofas with pillows and throws (but not so full that guests can't sit!) and create an atmosphere that is warm and welcoming for those you are inviting into your space.

Cozy spots and candles go hand in hand. Using items like vintage poufs, straw cushions, or just standard floor cushions not only makes your space feel a bit more welcoming, but they add visual interest and give the room more flavor and flair.

money that isn't sitting in my bank account, or the cool things I'm *not* doing. But focusing on those things blinds me to how full and wonderful my life actually is.

As I sat in that chair and heard the words coming out of my mouth, I realized that it was absolutely true. God had, at the moment, done something monumental in my heart. He'd once again worked out the kinks and made the crooked places of my heart straight.

I realized that day that God wasn't only speaking to me about myself and my life, but He was speaking to me about the presence of my friend and how good it was for me to have her in my life. Her mere presence gave Him the vehicle He needed to bring healing in my heart.

Friendships make life richer, better—they can turn black-and-white into Technicolor. If I were forced to choose between my absolute dream home filled with every beautiful thing I desired and a bank account flush with cash or living forever in a rental house but having a deep, wonderful, wide circle of friendships, I'd be happy to settle into that rental for eternity.

I don't think I can say it any better than Paul in 2 Corinthians:

Dear, dear Corinthians, I can't tell you how much I long for you to enter this wide-open, spacious life. We didn't fence you in. The smallness you feel comes from within you. Your lives aren't small, but you're living them in a small way. I'm speaking as plainly as I can and with great affection. Open up your lives. Live openly and expansively! (6:11–13 MSG)

We are not called to live small and lonely lives. We are not called to close ourselves off and focus only on our own families. We are called

to live in community. We are called to live big and to make friends with everyone around us. We are called to let each other in and love each other well.

Make room in your life for people, and you'll always be rich.

A LITTLE DEEPER | HOME + SOUL

Thank You, God, that my imperfections are perfected in You. Even when I am feeling the stress of trying to make my life and home perfect, I can rest in knowing that my true peace comes from You and the plan You have for my life and for the life of my family. In You, all things are made new. My old ways of thinking of myself and of the life You have given me have been washed by Your peace and covered in the hope that only You can bring. My hope is no longer found in material things or the way I impress others with what I have. I am not bound by cultural standards of happiness or richness; I now find my happiness in You. With that peace and strength, help me create a space and bring peace to my home that will have an everlasting effect on those who enter. Amen.

Make room in your life for people, and you'll always be rich. Your life will be full of His goodness, His grace, and His mercy through His people.

- If you had to choose between the perfect house and making wonderful, rich friendships, which would you choose? Are there ways in which you have actually had to make this choice?
- Think about the relationships in your life. If you were to "decorate your life" with these beautiful relationships, how would you make sure they take pride of place? Meet with others more often? In simpler ways? In more adventurous ways?
- Home-wise, how do you tend to be perfectionistic or feel inadequate about your stuff or the state of your home? How can you keep a motivation for order or tidiness from crossing over into something that prevents you from opening your home up others?

THE LET-GO LIST

You know the feeling: someone is coming for an impromptu visit, and you've only got a limited amount of time to get your welcome wagon ready. What do you do? Prioritize:

1   **A Place to Sit** | Clear off the couch, tables, breakfast bar, or anywhere you'll be sitting. ALL YOU NEED IS: a place for them to park it and a clean surface to set down their glass. DON'T WORRY ABOUT: the stuff of daily life that isn't perfectly organized and put away.

2   **Refreshments** | Take a second to put the kettle on (electric ones are my fave), mix up some quick lemonade or iced tea, or pop some cans or bottles in the fridge or freezer. A quick snack (like pretzels or rice crackers with hummus) in a bowl with some napkins is just fine. ALL YOU NEED IS: something wet to drink and something clean to put it in. DON'T WORRY ABOUT: dirty dishes you haven't gotten to yet (pile them in the sink and cover them with suds). Don't sweat chipped or mismatched cups or plates either.

3   **The Restroom** | Run a disinfecting wipe over the sink and over and under the toilet seat. Put out a fresh hand towel, make sure there's toilet paper, spritz some air freshener in the toilet, and give it a flush. Light a candle if you're feeling fancy. ALL YOU NEED IS: basic sanitation. DON'T WORRY ABOUT: chaos in your tub or bottles of lotions and potions; just pull the shower curtain or door. If you have a ton of clutter on the sink and other surfaces, put it in a laundry basket and set it in the tub before pulling the curtain, or pile it under your sink cabinet to quickly get it all out of the way.

CHAPTER 10

ENTERTAINING WITH STYLE + GRACE

A generous person will prosper;
whoever refreshes others will be refreshed.

—PROVERBS 11:25

One of things that I find most women are intimidated by when it comes to hosting a party is the idea that you have to have the best of everything to feel comfortable (there's that perfectionism at work again). Your house has to be perfectly decorated, your plates must be bone china and your napkins real linen, and your food has to be catered from the finest local restaurant. As much as I love fancy things, can we just go ahead and squelch that lie and put it to rest? Over the past seventeen years of entertaining, one thing I have discovered is that, at the end of the day, people don't care one bit how nice things are. They just want to have fun.

People don't care one bit how nice things are. They just want to have fun.

Hospitality is a unique and important purpose for your home. However you design it, God made your home to be opened and shared. Don't be intimidated by this, okay, friends? You've got this. With a few guidelines and fun tips, you're sure to be well on your way to hosting and opening up your home with the best of them.

Let's go through planning a gathering from beginning to end, shall we?

BUDGET

One of the first things you will want to consider is your budget. Whether you have hundreds to spend or less than fifty bucks, there's no doubt you can still set your event apart from others without breaking the bank. When planning your party, three areas tend to suck the life out of you and out of your budget.

DRINKS

Beverages open the window to our souls. Okay, I totally made that up, but no one, and I mean no one, wants to be thirsty. Ever. When entertaining, the more fun the drink, the better.

IF YOU CAN SPLURGE: Offering a wide range of beverages is key to making sure your party is a success. Don't be afraid to try something new. When setting up drinks at home, you'll want to put them out in an area that is easily accessible so folks can easily serve themselves. You can be a gracious host without hovering over people and keeping tabs on who needs a refill. Sit back, relax, and enjoy the fruits of your labor. Eat, laugh, and talk with those you've invited. When you're at ease, they will be as well. I like to offer both flat and sparkling water choices presented with bowls of lemon or lime wedges. There are so many fun ways you can add a little flavor not just to your drinks but also to your drink area. You don't have to use a cooler to hold sodas. Instead, pull out some of those flea market finds and think outside the cooler box. Once I filled an old rusty wheelbarrow with ice to hold Perrier water bottles. I just lined the inside with vinyl to avoid leaks! It was so much fun and sparked a lot of conversation between my guests and me. If your gathering is more formal, go for glasses. They add such a great touch, and water just tastes better out of a glass, am I right?

IF YOU'RE ON A TIGHTER BUDGET: If you don't have the funds to offer a wide variety of sodas, teas, and other drinks, you might want to consider a signature drink for your gathering. A delicious punch can be made easily and cheaply and served in pretty pitchers. I'd also recommend setting out some glass pitchers filled with ice and tap water in case punch isn't everyone's drink of choice!

FOOD

Food really makes or breaks a party. It's tough to have fun and connect when your stomach is rumbling and demanding pizza! If everyone is full

of delicious snacks and treats, I promise they will leave thinking your party was a success. Of course, it's important to have something for everyone to eat, even those with dietary limitations and needs.

IF YOU CAN SPLURGE: Make party planning easy on yourself and pick up a variety of appetizers and salads from your favorite restaurants around town. I like to stick to items that can be served cold, like chicken salad with crackers, deviled eggs, or shrimp cocktail; or items that reheat well, like bacon-wrapped figs. I will usually get one or two specialty salads—like a chopped salad and a caprese salad in the summer or a kale salad and a spinach and fruit salad in cooler months. My pro tip here is to ask for the salads deconstructed when you order them so they don't get soggy in your fridge before the party. Then right before the party, you can combine the ingredients and add dressing in a pretty bowl. Add a cheese board with a few specialty cheeses and sliced meats from your favorite upscale deli, and you have a nice variety of options. There is definitely a cost here, but this takes very little time, and you won't spend the whole party cooking or heating things up in the kitchen.

IF YOU'RE ON A TIGHTER BUDGET: You can still offer scrumptious foods without breaking the bank. Even with a tight budget, my goal is to make as much ahead of time as possible so I can enjoy the party—and food!—without spending the whole evening in the kitchen. I try to stick with a theme when I'm watching my pennies, since a cohesive menu can tie together less costly choices. For example, Mexican food is usually inexpensive. You can make a delicious queso in a small crockpot, which will keep it warm all evening, and pair it with bowls of tortilla chips and a variety of salsas. Set out some taco

DO IT TOGETHER!

When I'm hosting I like to designate secret cohosts—that's right, I said secret! These are friends no one is really aware will be cohosting with me. The sole purpose of these incognito hosts is to look for those who need to connect or aren't talking to anyone and pull them in. The aim is that no one gets left out when I'm hosting a gathering, and these secret cohosts are a huge help. I highly recommend you give this a try at your next party. Be sure to choose people who enjoy people and are naturally outgoing and talkative. Just about anyone can smell a fake, and there's nothing like disingenuous conversation to kill a party!

shells, shredded cheese, chopped green onions, shredded lettuce, and a bowl of ground beef for a make-your-own-taco bar. The only thing you'll have to make during the party is the ground beef—if you cook it ahead, just heat it up. Easy and inexpensive! You can do the same with a lot of different make-your-own bars. Make-your-own macaroni and cheese is always a hit in cold weather. A pot of basic mac and cheese with a variety of toppings like shredded cheddar, Gouda, and Swiss, as well as chopped green onions, chorizo, and bacon can make for a fun meal that even your youngest guests can enjoy.

TABLEWARE AND LINENS

Goodness. Lord knows that after food, this part's my favorite. Over the years I've definitely collected my fair share of forks, plates, bowls, napkins, and things that I don't even have names for that would fit into this category. This is another area where people typically give up, but it's one of the easiest and most fun areas to spice up your party and make it look like you put in a lot of work when you actually didn't.

Here are a few things it always helps to have on hand: simple white plates, a good set of flatware to service ten to twelve people, and cloth napkins. I love Crate & Barrel for these items, but you can find all of them at any price point. Target, Walmart, and Ikea all carry good options too! And don't forget thrift stores. I found my first set of white dishes at one, and to this day one of my favorite sets of vintage brass flatware came from a local thrift. Only vintage and antique items can add that sense of history and character to your table.

A GOOD TIME FOR A PARTY

You don't really need an excuse to have a party, but having an event to anchor to can help you get over any anxiety you might have about inviting new people over. It can also give you a handy theme.

+ HOLIDAYS | Apart from your standard calendar holidays, you might try some more obscure holidays or celebrations from faraway places. There's Bastille Day (crepes, anyone?), name days and saints' days, or something wacky like National Pie Day.

+ ENDINGS AND BEGINNINGS | Starting something new? Wrapping something up? Why not celebrate? Have a party to begin or end a semester or school year, calendar season (the first day of spring is always a reason to celebrate), group study, or class. Try a housewarming or a celebration for a new job or venture.

+ SEASONAL FOODS | God in His wisdom made certain foods amazing during certain seasons. If you have a particularly large bounty of strawberries or tomatoes in the summer, fresh fish or shellfish in season, spring vegetables, or winter cozy baking, it's a great reason to invite others over and share.

SETTING YOUR TABLE

After you've acquired your key elements—your drinks, your food, and your flatware—it's time to set the table. If you're hosting a larger gathering and not setting a table, that's fine. The following tips will work even in an intimate group of eight to ten or a larger gathering of even a hundred folks. If you're entertaining a lot of people, you will want to create "pockets" of conversation and set places for people to congregate and chat with one another as they please.

TABLECLOTHS | Unless you have a table that is in poor condition or are serving food you worry might damage your table, leave the table-cloths in the closet. Consider using a runner or placemats to add texture and character to the table. These are a little lower in maintenance and also don't get caught on the clothing of guests. If you're using a runner, think outside the box. You don't need to go to the store to purchase this. I've used scrap fabrics on many occasions and ripped them to leave raw edges and give the table a more natural and organic feel. I love a cozy and relaxed vibe when I am entertaining. You can also grab a large roll of Kraft paper and use that to cover your table. Then you can set food out and write what each plate contains right on the paper!

FLATWARE | Mix it up. Don't be afraid to combine or mix metals when setting the table. Remember, it does not need to be perfect to be fun, and everyone loves to feel unique and special. If you're really a go-getter, give everyone their own set (cue the thrift-store finds) and toss away the idea that they all have to be the same. This not only adds a bit of whimsy, but it also creates an atmosphere that is more relaxed and less stuffy. For a buffet-style serving situation, I recommend wrapping a napkin around each set of silverware and tying it off with a bit of ribbon or twine and putting them all in a pail or basket at the end of the buffet. That way, each guest can grab a set of silverware and a plate and get to eating without having to fumble for each individual utensil.

LAYERS | Whether you use a tablecloth or a runner, a placemat or a charger, layers are your friend. Start from the bottom up with the last layer being your flatware. The more you layer elements on the table, even if your goal is simplicity, the more beautiful your table will look. It doesn't take a lot of effort either. That can be your little secret. No one needs to know that you didn't expend countless hours of energy to get it just right. Alternatively, if giving your table as much movement and personality is your goal, adding name cards atop plates or beside them, using greenery and flowers as your runner, or featuring a patterned accent plate/charger or tablecloth are all ways that you can give your table that extra bit of personality.

FLORALS | Nothing brings more life to a table than live things, and nothing is more visually pleasing. One thing to consider before placing

A LITTLE DEEPER | HOME + SOUL

God, thank You for making us creatures of community, and for building my heart to connect with those You've put in my life. I want to join You in healing, enriching, and refreshing others when I welcome them into my home. Please give me opportunities, ideas, and excuses to let people in and bring them together. After all, You are the Creator of fun! I pray that when we come together, You'll be there with us.

florals on your table is whether any of your guests may have allergies to any blooms you may be considering. One way to combat this is by replacing your blooms with greens like eucalyptus. Not only are they sometimes even more beautiful and simple, they are often a lot less expensive. If your budget is too tight for a florist, try club stores like Costco or even your local grocery stores. When shopping local grocers just ensure that they are sourcing, if at all possible, through local growers and farmers.

Setting your table and home for people to enter does not have to be stressful. Remember that you're doing just what you've been created to do. It's part of what your home was created for too. Home should be a place that brings peace and comfort to those who enter, and especially those who are broken and hurting. It's one of the ways God shares His comfort—through us and our welcome. When we design our homes around this purpose, we partner with Christ to bring redemption and restoration to the lives of others.

> Home should be a place that brings peace and comfort to those who enter, and especially those who are broken and hurting.

So kick back and enjoy the people around you. You were meant for it. Now you're one step closer to filling those hearts and your home with the grace, love, and *fun* you were intended to have all along.

REFLECT

- Think about a few of the best parties you've been to, be they weddings, home gatherings, or formal affairs. What little details did you find delightful?

- Who in your life can you bring onto your party team? Who would make a good cohost? Who can you invite whom you'd like to get to know better?

- How have you been healed through community and hospitality from other people? How can you become a healer too?

CHAPTER 11

GATHERING IN ALL SEASONS

Let us consider how we may spur one another on toward love and good deeds, not giving up meeting together, as some are in the habit of doing, but encouraging one another—and all the more as you see the Day approaching.

—HEBREWS 10:24–25

There's nothing I love more than the anticipation and the welcoming in of each season.

I don't know if I can choose any one season as my favorite. Each and every season carries a uniqueness that the one prior just cannot compete with. We hold fast to the dog days of summer with all our might as the cool winds of autumn bring us the most remarkable colors in nature we ever did see. Then comes winter with its cool and crisp air and, if we're lucky enough, a few snow days. And spring. Where would we be without spring? It brings the hope and promise of things to come.

When it comes to entertaining or hosting, each season offers a chance for different types of gatherings. I know it can be difficult to pull yourself out of your cozy cocoon during the cold, snowy months to throw a dinner party, but it's worth it. Fall can get so busy with shorter days, back-to-school activities, and sports that it can be hard to break routine and plan a party. But it's worth it. Even spring and summer, with longer days and a more relaxed vibe, can begin to feel too hectic for entertaining between travel, camps and swim lessons, and rainy weather, but, again, it's worth it. God is calling you to create community year-round.

God is calling you to create community year-round.

WINTER

I consider winter to be prime real estate for entertaining—perhaps, in part, because I live in the Pacific Northwest and we have to get creative in the winter around here with just about everything in life. There is so much to capitalize on during this season. Unlike summer, you won't be entertaining outside, unless you live in a location that boasts a tropical climate. Winter is the perfect time of year for more intimate dinner parties. Invite a few new friends and let the cool weather outside and cozy atmosphere inside guide you to deeper conversations that turn new friends into dear friends. One of the best parts of winter is the abundance of holidays—Christmas, New Year's Eve, Valentine's Day—all worth celebrating!

Recently I hosted a Christmas party with a group of ladies in our home. We exchanged white elephant gifts, ate really good food, and crafted handmade wreaths that would make even Martha proud. (Martha Stewart that is—not Martha of Martha and Mary, although that Martha probably would have liked them too!) We had thirty women in only about five hundred square feet. Don't let lack of space present a limitation for you. Be determined that "if you build it, they will come." I have found this true over and over again in the area of entertaining. Our current home is tiny—and I long for the day when I'll have a bigger space so I can include more people in my gatherings, but I'm not waiting until that day to invite others into my life and home. Women are hungry for community and relationship, and, even in a super small space, you can be the one to bring these things to the people whom you live among and do life with.

SPRING

This may be everyone's favorite. Not too hot. Not too cold. Just right. Whether it's an Easter brunch or an outdoor party in the backyard, spring beckons to each and every one of us to enjoy the fruits of our labor stored away over the fall and winter. When organizing a party for the spring, you'll want to consider these five essentials as you plan:

SIMPLE TABLE COVERINGS AND CENTERPIECES | Keep it simple. For your next outdoor party, consider using craft or butcher paper, which can be purchased online or at your local packaging store

for a low cost, to cover your tables. The fun part? Guests can write on it and leave notes for the host with chalk paint pens or wax pencils. Talk about multifunctional. And who doesn't love receiving words of affirmation from others?

FUN VASES FOR FLOWERS | For centerpieces, hop back on that thrift store train and look for pitchers or other vessels you can use in simple ways to add character and flair. Vintage pitchers or even handmade clay pots are perfect stand-ins for your ordinary glass vase.

CASUAL DRINK STATION | Who says you need only one? No one likes standing in line for things. If you have a larger party, consider creating more than one beverage station to suit the crowd you are entertaining. This will eliminate crowding and free up space for more conversation, while also creating an atmosphere that is more peaceful and less convoluted. When creating your casual drink station—whether for water or otherwise—beverage dispensers make things easier for guests. Pro tip: for those pesky drink dispensers that leak no matter what, try using a hot glue gun to seal off the spout from the inside. This should help in eliminating those endless drips and make everyone serving themselves a little bit happier.

OUTDOOR DINING AREA | When planning your gathering, be sure to consider the time of day you'll be hosting and the placement of tables and chairs. You'll want to be mindful of where the sun hits and how to avoid having sun in your guests' eyes. If the area you are in has full sun no matter where you are, and your budget allows, consider purchasing sunglasses or visors for everyone (Amazon or Oriental Trading Co. work wonders for bulk purchases) and setting them out in baskets. Your guests will love the idea, guaranteed, and who doesn't love a free spare pair of sunglasses to keep in the glove compartment? You win.

They win. We all win. I'd also recommended putting out a few bottles of environmentally friendly or natural bug spray (eucalyptus oil is one of my faves) and sunscreen for guests to use if needed!

5-Minute Natural Bug Repellent with Essential Oils

Ingredients:

30 drops citrus oil (orange/lemon)

30 drops eucalyptus essential oil

20 drops lavender essential oil

1 Tablespoon rubbing alcohol

½ cup witch hazel

½ cup water or vinegar

1 teaspoon vegetable glycerin (optional)

Directions:

+ Place essential oils in an amber glass bottle (can be ordered via online bulk retailer) with alcohol, and shake well to combine.

+ Add witch hazel and shake.

+ Add vegetable glycerin (optional).

+ Add water (or vinegar). Shake again.

ECO-FRIENDLY DISPOSABLES | Somehow, I always lose way more things when entertaining outdoors—utensils get dropped and lost in bushes or plates break. For a small group, it's easier to keep tabs on everything, but for a large group, you may want to consider disposable plates, napkins, cups, and cutlery. There are so many eco-friendly options available these days that allow you to go easy on your wallet while not skimping on style, including bamboo, other wood, paper, and fiber. Most grocers (and definitely some specialty grocers) will carry these eco-friendly options.

SUMMER

All year long we long for this season, when life is a little more relaxing, days are longer, and there is so much sun. There's nothing more enticing than summer entertaining on the beach, at the park, or even in your own backyard. The possibilities with summer entertaining are virtually endless, but here are a few tips and techniques to set you on your way.

THE HOUR MATTERS | The rest of the year is perfect for morning brunches or luncheons, but summer is all about the late afternoon and evening. With summer kickin' the heat to us in most locations, shift the time of your party from midday to sunset. It will still be warm enough for outdoor entertaining, but not so hot that your guests spend the whole party sweating.

GRILL IT | Give your oven a rest and pull out your grill for quick and easy dining. Hamburgers and hotdogs are always crowd pleasers, but kick it up a notch by allowing guests to add their own flavors and seasoning to their burgers (with your glove-handed help, of course). Rosemary, basil pesto, and aged soft cheeses are always great to add a little life to an ordinary burger. Pair those grilled goodies with simple bowls of chips and cut-up fruit for the perfect summer meal.

MAKE IT FUN | Summer is the perfect season for outdoor play! Hide and seek, flashlight tag, and even Red Rover are all fun for kids. Cool off and let your kids let loose with water. No pool? No problem. Fill

up buckets with small water balloons in advance of the party and let the kids have a water-balloon fight. Or buy up some inexpensive water guns at your local dollar store for a game of tag. Want simple? Grab a Slip 'N' Slide and let the kids go nuts. They will have fun and wear themselves out for an easy bedtime!

For the adults, a little cornhole, spike ball, or bocce ball will add entertainment to make everyone happy. Top it all off with a bonfire and s'mores and you're collecting memories that will last a lifetime.

AUTUMN

Cooler weather, crisp breezes, and shorter days usher in this season. Kids get back into a rhythm of school days and life gets more structured. You'll want to take advantage of indoors and outdoors during this season. If you live somewhere chillier, host a bonfire party with fancy s'mores making. Stock up on lots of fleece blankets and serve hot apple cider so everyone can snuggle around the fire.

If it's too cold for outside, host indoors and make s'mores around the fireplace or over the stovetop. Drape furniture with fuzzy throws and add sheepskin rugs and large floor pillows around the fire to add a bit of warmth and make things a little cozier. Light lots of candles to combat the darkness outside at this time of year. It's easy to find inexpensive votive candles in various heights and sizes. Just pop them into glass vases and containers to set the mood. Fall is also perfect for themed parties. Back to school, football, harvest—there are so many fun options!

———

No matter what time of year it is, there is always a chance to invite others into your home and foster the relationships God wants you to have.

A LITTLE DEEPER | HOME + SOUL

God, You steer our lives through each year, giving us good gifts that perfectly complement the seasons. Thank You for this cycle of comforts and joys. Show us how to celebrate them and You together as we move through the year, praising You for the simple things and enjoying them fully. Please bless us as we find new things to love about each other and Your world with each passing month.

REFLECT

- Think about the best get-togethers you've been to for each season. What made them so special? How did they complement the season?
- What foods, feelings, and textures do you most look forward to for each season? How can you work those into your space this coming year?
- Get out your calendar and look for time to have one get-together per season this year, no matter how big or small. Planning ahead gives you time to commit and make it special. What seasonal comforts will you enjoy together?

A SEASONAL TABLE

Some seasonal treats not only taste good but look great on a table. Consider using them to fill pottery bowls, adorn mantles, or freshen up a console table instead of flowers. You might fare better at a local farmers market where you can ask the source what's in season and pick up character-filled items that a grocery store might not carry. Here are a few ideas as pleasing to the eye as they are to the palate.

WINTER

Brussels sprouts on the stalk (these pieces are downright sculptural)

Clementines in a marble or wooden bowl (snackable and pleasing)

Cranberries in a tall glass vase

Pomegranates

SPRING

Fresh herbs growing in pots

Artichokes

Pepper plants

Lemons

Purple sprouting broccoli

SUMMER

Nectarines and stone fruit

Rainbow chard

Berries

Any big baskets of bounty from the garden

Heirloom tomatoes

Fresh figs

FALL

Pumpkins and gourds

Apples (try them hollowed out with little votive candles in them)

Dried corn

Colorful carrots

Colorful kale

Pears

SEASONAL ADDITIONS

When changing out seating and eating areas for seasonal gatherings,
I find that a few colors, fabrics, materials, and textures lend themselves
to a seasonal feel. Try experimenting with throws, pillows, accessories,
and tableware that signal the season. They're easy to swap out as the
year progresses.

+ WINTER | fur and sheepskin, wool, fleece, flannel, velvet, beeswax
    candles, deep jewel tones, evergreens, juniper berries, dark wood,
    antlers, brass, plaid

+ SPRING | bamboo, cotton, loose knitted or crocheted items, greys
    and muted pastels, rattan, raffia, floral or botanical patterns, fresh
    flowers

+ SUMMER | linen, raw silk blends, netting or lace, grass baskets or
    woven items, light colored wood, glazed pottery, white crockery,
    textured glass, checked fabric, whites and brights, succulents, heat-
    loving wildflowers

+ FALL | flannel, burlap, wicker, dried flowers, wheat, mason jars,
    heavy crockery, uniquely shaped gourds, rich browns and earth
    tones like rusts or golden colors

CHAPTER 12

INVITE OTHERS IN

They broke bread in their homes and ate together with
glad and sincere hearts.

—ACTS 2:46

Some of the most important lessons I have learned in life have come through those whom God has blessed me to live in community with. Sometimes when I've least expected it, a hello in the hallway has turned into a lifetime friendship with the best of people who have supported me through the good and bad seasons of life.

There's nothing more powerful than embracing the beauty of the collective story of those around you and gathering to fuel the fires of one another. I absolutely live for it. And our homes are made for it.

Friend, not only are we not meant to live life alone, I believe, aside from Jesus Christ Himself, that fellowship is truly the oxygen to our lungs and one of the primary reasons we've been placed on this earth.

The world we live in is full of so many demands, and we tend to live quite superficially. We go from place to place, running errands, taking care of things, living in the cult of busy, and never truly connecting with those we encounter on a daily basis. I believe life is meant for so much more. I know it is.

God always finds a way to connect us, even when we don't want to be connected. He is intentional. Even when we would rather have our lives all sorted and figured out to our personal preferences, thank you very much, He pursues us with the golden promise of more and better. He chases after our hearts in a way that beckons our very souls. I know it, because He did it with me. He did it by teaching me to open up my home to my community. In the messy times and in the times of celebration, our lives are so much richer when we invite people in.

COMMUNITY FINDS US

I made a commitment to myself a few years into my life as a military wife: I would grow where we'd been planted, even if it was temporary, and foster true relationships no matter how challenging it may be. We'd invite people over, and we'd potluck at others' homes. We'd leave our kids for playdates and take on the adventure of game nights and all sorts of other activities in and outside our homes.

Every three years it was time to pack up and do it all over again. My heart always hurt for the people we'd be leaving behind, and I'd hope that we'd be lucky enough to see them on our next assignment. That rarely happened.

In our next place, I'd sow the same seeds. We were committed to wholeheartedly diving into whatever community we were placed in and

There's nothing more powerful than
embracing the beauty of the collective
story of those around you and gathering to
fuel the fires of one another.

connecting with those around us. Still, with each move, it got harder and harder to finally get comfortable in our new space. I felt like I was always restless, never able to relax, because I knew the orders would come and we'd be moving again.

I think this was a normal feeling to have, but, for me, it became an agitation that sat on my heart like a bag of elephants. It all came to a head during our last year in Hawaii, when we learned Larry would be deployed to Afghanistan that entire year. I was pregnant with our youngest son and scared silly at the thought of my husband fighting overseas. Life got real and heavy really fast.

I did what any decent woman would do in this type of situation: I cried. Then I put my big girl pants on and decided that I would do things differently than I'd done in the past. We would have to move to the base from our home in town while Larry was away, and I needed to decide to do this with the right attitude.

Instead of working nonstop to make things feel a certain way in our home or look good immediately after the moving truck left, I would choose to completely trust and rest in God to fulfill the needs and wants of my heart and to transform our home from the inside out. For us, that came through community. When things were far from perfect, in our home and in life, beauty came through letting others in.

When things were far from perfect, in our home and in life, beauty came through letting others in.

5 MUST-HAVES FOR
OVERNIGHT GUESTS

One of the easiest ways to make guests feel even more at home and welcome when they are away from their own home is by adding personal touches that let them know that you are happy they came. Here are a few ways I've welcomed guests into our home:

1. **A Basket of Goodies** | Even better is to stack it full of your guests' favorite things. Large or small, you choose. I always like to include toiletry items as well just in case they forget something. Disposable razors, soap, and deodorant are all good items to start with.

2. **Wi-Fi Codes + Passwords** | This one's pretty self-explanatory, but when you have a list accessible to them from the beginning, they don't have to ask for it, and you have one less thing to worry about relaying to guests.

3. **Water Pitcher** | Seems pretty simple and maybe even unnecessary, but I get pretty parched at night, and nothing is worse than having to wake up, slide on my house slippers (or even worse, go in bare feet), and walk to the fridge to grab a sip of water when I am a guest in someone else's home. There are so many options that come with cups that cover the openings, which is a win for me, as they keep the creepy crawlers at bay and my water good and fresh until morning.

4. **Sounds** | For our family, Bluetooth and Wi-Fi speakers are all the rage, and our kids don't sleep without the sound of smooth tunes

or white noise in the background to lull them to sleep. While some may want complete silence while they sleep, others may enjoy the sound of soft music. Honestly, even if they don't, who doesn't love to have a little peppy pick-me-up of jazz or other sounds in their room to entertain them during waking hours? Out of the five things listed here, this one may be my favorite. Search online for Wi-Fi speakers that are right for your home and budget.

5 **Personal Throw Blanket** | You don't need to go as far as monogramming your guests' initials on the blanket, but I do love the idea of guests having something to take away with them to remember their stay in our home. You don't need cashmere money either. With this one, it's really the thought that counts, and, trust me, your thought will go a long way here. If you know the color palette in your guests' home or their favorite color, go for that. They'll have cozy memories for years to come as they snuggle up with this special parting gift. If the season just doesn't seem right for a throw, consider gifting a woven basket or container of some sort that can be used in the home as well. The sky really is the limit depending on your budget, and you have permission to be extremely creative.

GOODBYE TO THE ONE-WOMAN SHOW

I was exhausted, pregnant, and at my limit when I moved three kids from our rental on one side of the island to the base on the other side of the island. During that time I realized I needed the help of those around me more than ever before. As much as I tried to avoid it, I ended up not only asking for help, but taking every drop of help I could get from those who'd offered time and time again.

If you've ever been to Hawaii, you'll know that the culture of locals on-island will put even Southern hospitality to shame. This "shirt off your back" attitude was one that I came to know and love. From cleaning my house, to keeping me company, and even watching my kids while I had time to myself, our church community showered me with the gifts of time and love. They gave me a new perspective of just how fulfilling it was to spend time with those I love and give whatever I could to those in need. In entering my home and welcoming me into theirs, they showed me what a beautiful cycle of giving and receiving could take place when we open our doors.

I cannot imagine how much different my life would look today without having their sacrifice of love as an example. They gave of themselves relentlessly and without thought or care of any consequence. To this day, those women who dragged me (sometimes kicking and screaming) into their lives and held me up when I was sinking are like sisters to me. It's such a precious thing that I have to ask: Why did I ever resist? Why do we resist community, especially when it's in our homes?

I'd always been pretty independent when it came to receiving help and doing things on my own. But during that season, I needed people to surround me with the type of love and genuine care I'd so often felt was for others but not for me.

Why not for me? I've always been the helper. I grew up watching women in my life whom I looked up to always helping others. I never witnessed any of them in a vulnerable situation. While they taught me invaluable life skills and lent a hand in training me in the ways of generous living, they also inadvertently taught me that I could do all things on my own. I never felt the need to ask for help for anything as a child, and this festered as I became an adult. Perhaps I perceived *my* needing help as a weakness. When *others* needed help, it seemed normal. When I needed help, it felt bad. God took that from me in Hawaii.

This time, making this home, it was my turn. It was my turn to open up and lean in to all that God wanted to do in my life through these people, through this mess. As much as I tried to fight it, there was just no way to shut down the miracle God wanted to perform for me and my kids. He was ready to show me what it really meant to live life *with* others in true community. He was restoring us with His love and showing us what a restored, open, vulnerable home looked like.

Up until this point, I always thought I was okay pushing through on my own—better than okay, even. I think sometimes we're so bent on doing things the way we have always done them, we don't realize what we're missing.

I had been trying to one-woman-show my way through the process of establishing each home when I didn't need to. He was offering me a new life in community. A new life of not only giving but receiving. I could rest in knowing that He was in control and that, no matter where we physically landed, what our house looked like, or how perfectly decorated and styled it was on the inside, I could trust Him to do the work of turning every house we occupied into a *home*.

GET HELP

Some things are just better with friends and neighbors. Beyond the usual, such as moving furniture and painting walls, here are a few ideas to take you out of the one-woman-show mind-set and bring you deeper into community while making your home.

+ FLEA MARKET FRIENDSHIP | Two pairs of eyes are better than one, especially when you're digging through piles at a flea market, garage sale, or secondhand shop. And even more especially if your friend has bargaining skills!

+ THE BARTER | If you and a friend (or a group) have any design or functional woes in your home, don't hold back. Share with each other, and take it to the next level by signing on to help do something about it. You can trade time and effort, with your many hands making lighter work. Maybe you can trade some flat-pack closet help for assistance with putting up a new backsplash. Feed off one another's inspiration and fresh perspective.

+ FRIENDLY FORAGERS | In your backyard, the woods, or a friend's place, ask for company in bringing the outdoors in. It could be combing the beach for some good stones, searching the woods for antlers, or finding green foliage in overgrown places.

A HOME FOR COMMUNITY

We can't often control where community finds us, whether we're struggling through a cross-country move, jump-starting a random conversation with a stranger in the grocery store checkout line, or filling up our gas tank with a new buddy on the other side of the pump. What we *can* do is control how we foster community in our homes. It's the one place where we can set the tone and pace for conversations of a lifetime to take place. This is the place where we give of ourselves and where we receive the gifts of friendship.

When you have built up a restored home, fostering community in your home becomes your mission. You will live for the moments that create memories and that fill the hearts of others. You will encourage genuine and authentic connection and friendship with grace. You won't do it so that people can rant and rave about how beautiful your home is or how much you spent on food. You won't do it so that the world can know

REFLECT

- In what ways is it difficult for you to ask for or accept help? How can you begin to push through that in small ways?
- Are there ways in which you resist community? What good might come from giving up that resistance?
- In what ways can you commit to diving into your community? How can your home be a tool to help make that happen?

MAKE IT PERSONAL

Consider writing a personal note to those visiting with you, letting them know how excited you are to have them and some of the things you are looking forward to doing with them during their stay. You are setting the tone for them to feel accepted and loved from the beginning, and it's guaranteed to feed your heart as well.

Life is full, and things get busy, especially if you have children, but you can make them a part of the party by having them write something in the card to guests as well. If your kids aren't old enough to write just yet, ask them what they'd like to say and write it for them. An alternative to this paper form of gratitude is to whip out the handy dandy cell phone and record a video that your guests can watch. Just send it off to them before they arrive.

how well you entertain or how immaculate your living room is. You'll do it for eternity. You'll do it with full purpose, knowing that doing so restores you too.

This is community—restored. This is how we fill one another's cups. This is how our hearts become full and how we pour out, continually, from one person to another. And this is how we never get enough.

Home is a place to host many things: people, events, family, and friends. These gatherings create a sense of togetherness and community that is essential for healthy and whole living.

For me and my family, community has been a lifeline to the fulfillment of purpose. Life gathered with people, even if it feels a little vulnerable, risky, or messy, is a life much richer, deeper, more meaningful, and impactful. Life without those relationships leaves us quickly feeling dried out, empty, and searching for meaning.

> Life gathered with people, even if it feels a little vulnerable, risky, or messy, is a life much richer, deeper, more meaningful, and impactful.

In the beginning, we see that God created man and then woman. He created them for the purpose of communing—of having a relationship with Him and a relationship with one another.

We know the rest of that story and how it ends—God used His own Son to come down and restore us, by living in community with us. God's restorative plan continues through us. We all get to partake in this miraculous plan using our homes as foundations for bringing to life the story of redemption through community.

His heart for us has always been relationship. His heart for our lives is that we would choose to commit ourselves to Him and to one another, and that we would enjoy the connectedness that fellowship brings in homes with open doors.

A LITTLE DEEPER | HOME + SOUL

God, thank You for placing me in this community, in this time and place. Teach me how to embrace the people in my community in my home, to give to them and receive from them, and to welcome the blessings that come when we gather together. Open my eyes to see how I can make my home one that nurtures, treasures, and encourages connection. I invite You, and the people You gave me, in.

EXTENDED INVITATIONS

Hosting overnight guests can be a vulnerable and beautiful invitation into your home life, if even for a night or a few days. There are plenty of ways to make guests feel right at home with a few simple touches.

+ Flowers on the coffee table, in the kitchen, or even in the bathroom can set people at ease, and the aroma adds even more of a special touch. It may be good to ask beforehand if they have any allergies. They will be thankful you asked.

+ Guests always appreciate plenty of towels at the ready for hand drying or, for extended stays, in a basket in the bathroom or guest room they will be using along with soaps and lotions to make their stay a little easier.

+ To help them stay connected with home, try welcome cards printed with your contact details, Wi-Fi network and password, or other passwords or codes they might need.

+ Set out a few local guidebooks or maps to help them enjoy the area if they want to explore. You could even add a list of your favorite local attractions and eateries.

+ Set out some bottled water or a carafe and glass to keep them hydrated (if they're shy about stumbling to the kitchen at night for water), along with some local snacks or chocolates for late-night noshing.

+ Tissues, extra blankets, candles and matches, magazines or favorite books, and a comfy chair in their area can help them have a cozy moment to themselves.

PLANS + DREAMS

By now, I hope you've begun to embrace new plans and dreams for your restored home, knowing the beautiful purposes God has for it. From restoring your story, to a place for your home life, to a place for community, so much beauty can be born within those four walls. You might think that the God of the universe has more important things to do than to hear about your home or your decorating ideas. But friend, I want to assure you that God deals with the heart, and the heart of the child He loves. (That's you and me, by the way.) If it's in your heart to build a place of joy in your home, He wants to hear about it. If you want a space that is pleasing not just to the eye but also to the soul, He'll take it to levels you never would have imagined. He desires to go above and beyond your wildest dreams not just in what you consider the big things in your life but also in the details of your home.

While I'd devoted my time to the superficial in my home all those years, God was doing what He does best. He was carrying me. He was walking with me. Through each and every unsettled season and internal struggle, He was bringing me back home over and over again. Back to the home of my heart. He was bringing me to a new place of understanding not just that home was a representation of safety and love, void of fear; He was reassuring me and teaching me that the foundation of that truth had been solidified in the connection of my home and His love for me.

In Him, we find a safe place. In Him there is no fear. In Him is beauty and comfort and joy, and *that* revelation changed everything about the way that I viewed what our homes actually represent this side of heaven.

Here's how He works:

> Mortals make elaborate plans,
> but GOD has the last word.
> Humans are satisfied with whatever looks good;
> GOD probes for what is good.
> Put GOD in charge of your work,
> then what you've planned will take place.
> (Proverbs 16:1–3 MSG)

For so long, I felt such an unhealthy tension between my work and God's that no peace could reside in that place. When I desired the superficial things, He gently reminded me what actually mattered in life and specifically in our home. There might be a healthy tension in that space until the day I die, but I know it allowed me to grow. It taught me I didn't have to fight to make something *be* what it already was. Our home wasn't just ours—it was His. The day I decided to commit my work and my dreams and plans and ideas about what that should look like completely to Him was the day I experienced a freedom like never before.

All the plans I'd made were futile. But when we shift and make those plans for our dream home (including kitchen, bathroom, bedroom, and den) *with* Him—when we dream *with* Him—all of those plans and dreams start to line up with His reality and His plans for our lives. This has been my story, friend, and I am pretty sure that if you haven't experienced this in your life already, it will be for you too.

I want to encourage you again to pray over your plans and dreams for your home. I feel a little ridiculous telling you to pray over your Pinterest boards, but I'm sure people have prayed over weirder things!

The thing is, God wants to be invited into the creation of your home. He cares deeply about the details and wants to be intimately involved in creating something beautiful *with* you. So give Him all your ideas. Give Him all your worries and your doubts and your fears as well. Go ahead and tell Him about that perfect light fixture or your desire to give your living room a modern farmhouse vibe. And listen. Listen for those little nudges that tell you you're on track. Also, don't be afraid to ask Him for *His* ideas. Our Father is intensely present in all aspects of our lives, large and small. As you place Him at the center of your restored home, you'll find yourself, and all those who enter, restored—heart and soul.

ACKNOWLEDGMENTS

It would be remiss of me not to take a moment here at the end of all of this to speak a word of gratitude and thankfulness to the women who helped pave the way for me. I know I mentioned them very briefly at the beginning of all of this, but it's not until now that I realize just how heavy a hand one of them had in sharing the weight of this with me even though she is no longer with me—my grandmother.

I never called her that. She was "memaw" and was a woman of great strength and one who unknowingly fulfilled great purpose in my life far beyond what she would ever set out to or even imagine she could do.

I truly believe, if not for her, I'd know nothing of community or what home truly means. She was an effortless host and lover of people and reflected the simplicity of knowing that sometimes (read: all the time) the most simple and uncomplicated things in life are the best things in life. She never tried to do this—it was just who she was. Because of her willingness to embrace what had been placed in her as a gift to us all, I am able to run wholeheartedly into what I know God has also freely and graciously placed in me.

My heart swells as I think of all the possibilities this book may open up in the hearts and minds of people across the world. It swells even more as I imagine how the revelation of the truth that this message holds will bring freedom and how it has the power to propel each of us into a movement to see ourselves, our homes, and those who enter them in a way we never have before. It is both a sobering and joy-filled thought and a truth that is not lost on me.

Even more weighty is the thought that my "memaw" had a small part to play in hosting this conversation long before it was ever a hope in my own heart. I'd like to think that maybe she saw something in me. A key that I held to carrying on something special and that would unlock the door for many to also receive.

There were many who had a part to play in this, of course. Those who picked up the torch well after my grandmother laid hers down.

To my aunts and my uncle | thank you for loving me and supporting me—always.

To Molly (the one who started this crazy adventure for me with a simple e-mail) and Whitney | thank you for seeing something in me and calling it out and setting it on fire.

To my husband, Larry, and to my kids Caleb, Kendall, Logan and Grayson | thank you for allowing me to be imperfect and for teaching me to lean in to the one *Great Perfecter* and helping me to see Him in each of you. I love you.

To my friends—you know exactly who you are | Thank you for riding this out with me, for seeing me and for encouraging me when I didn't see the end in it all. You are my heroes.

To my Restoration House community—the ones I've yet to see or even really know | thank you for over ten years of support. For the laughs and the tears. The truths and the fears. And everything in between. Restoration House would not hold true meaning or purpose without each of you.

SOURCES + CREDITS

PHOTOGRAPHY BY TIARRA SORTE

www.tiarrasorte.com

FEATURED VENDORS

Thanks to the following business for supporting the completion of this project:

Thimble & Cloth

www.thimbleandcloth.com

The Grit and Polish

www.thegritandpolish.com

Oscar and Co.

Seattle, Washington

FEATURED DECOR

Pages 7, 12 | Shoe Lasts | Oscar and Co., Seattle

Page 10 | Linen Napkin | Crate & Barrel

Page 11 | Vintage Paintbrushes | Oscar and Co., Seattle

Page 25 | Throw Pillows | Thimble & Cloth

Page 65, 66 | Wooden Bowl | World Market

Page 67 | Vintage Pitcher and Glass Beads | vintage finds

Page 105 | Dining chairs | Thimble & Cloth

ABOUT THE AUTHOR

KENNESHA BUYCKS is the creator of Restoration House. A Southern transplant to the Pacific Northwest, she has a passion for connecting others, gathering, and inspirational styling and design. When Kennesha is not busy being a wife to her amazing husband or a mama to her four kids, she spends her time writing, blogging, and encouraging others to live life uniquely and with passion. Find her online at RestorationHouseBlog.com and on Instagram @restorationhouse.

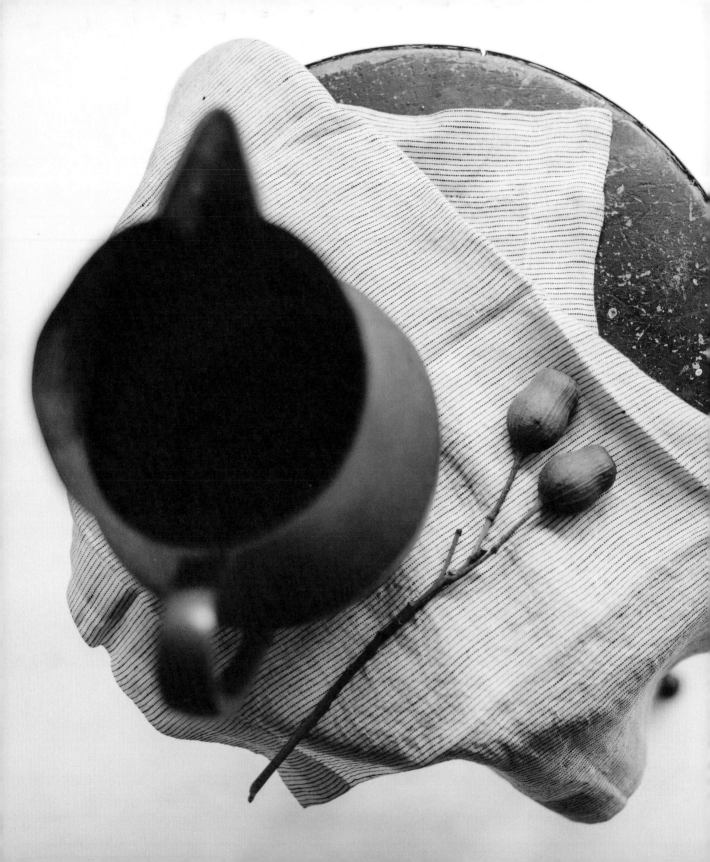